The

Ocotillo

Review

Volume 7.1

Winter 2023

The Ocotillo Review Volume 7.1

Attention Schools and businesses: For discounted prices on large orders please contact the publisher directly.

Kallisto Gaia Press Inc.
1801 E. 51st Street
Suite 365-246
Austin TX 78723
info@kallistogaiapress.org
(254) 654-7205

Cover Design: Tony Burnett
Edited by Tony Burnett

ISSN: 2573-4113
ISBN: 978-1-952224-31-7

The Ocotillo Review

Volume 7.1
The Alternative Family

Winter 2023

FICTION - POETRY - TRUTH

Table of Contents

Poetry

1	It could have happened otherwise	M. Ann Reed
9	Heritage	Karan Kapoor
10	sleep: fragments	Karan Kapoor
13	aubade	Karan Kapoor
14	Try Harder	Jennifer MacKenzie
15	Sensus Fidelium	Jennifer MacKenzie
20	Looking to the Stars	Ann Howells
21	On an Evening Walk by the Texas State Lunatic Asylum Cemetery	Greta Rasmus
22	Amor Mortis	Charles Brice
23	Spin	Charles Brice
29	Appreciate Worms	Cassady O'Reilly-Hahn
36	The Intersection	Lawrence Bridges
37	The Spitting Wind	Lawrence Bridges
38	More Than us, but Less than Wind	Millicent Borges Accardi
39	Whoever You Are	T K Edmond
49	Some Far Star	John Bradley
50	The Color of War	John Bradley
51	Behind a Locked Door: Brief Interview with Covid-19	Johm Bradley
52	Dear Bog Man	John Bradley
53	The Weather On Mars	John Bradley
84	The Mulch	Oisin Breen
85	The System	Bart Edelman
86	What It Takes	Lynn Gilbert
87	Regardless	Lynn Gilbert
97	The Jesus Bed	Daaniel Moore

5 Ghazals

98	In Love	Shannan Mann
99	For God	Shannan Mann
100	Family	Shannan Mann
101	Foind	Shannan Mann
102	The Pain	Shannan Mann
111	Somewhere In America	Scott Lowery
118	Thoughts at 2:30 a.m.	Kaitlyn Bankroft
119	In Which I Loved You In the Desert	Kaaitlyn Bankroft
120	Soccer	Hilary Sideris
121	Coney Island Avenue	Hilary Sideris
122	Mannheim Traain Station at Midnight	Michael Hardin
123	Swim Meet	Michael Hardin
128	Friends	Stephen Campiglio

135	In Which I Unthinkingly Meet the Eye of a Homeless Woman in the Park	Devon Balwit
144	The Hair on the Wall of the Shower	Amanda Hoffman
145	Anatomy of the United States of America	James Mathis
155	The Poems of Our Climate	Benjamin Green
156	Octopuses and Old Age	Claire Rubin
168	Little Wind	Bruce McRae
169	One Night In Ten	Bruce McRae
170	A Little Chat with Oneself	Bruce McRae
171	Disappearing Act	Karlie Powers
179	Refuge	Alfred Fournier
181	What Made Him Eat	Michael Foran
182	Aunt Margie's Magic Book	Richard Matta
183	The Outside Is Endless	Paul Koniecki
193	Hair	Jen McClanaghan
196	Oil and Nectar	Ashley Schnidt
197	What If the Roses Don't Smell	Eva Nemirovsky
199	The Lesson	Christian Paulisich
200	Al Dente'	Christian Paulisich
201	Secondary	Merie Kirby
202	One Year In Every Ten I Manage It	Christine Hamm
203	Doll Parts	Christine Hamm

Fiction

3	Elbow-Length Gloves	R.w. Meeks
17	Caring For Her	Rosalind Goldsmith
24	Dreams	Peter Stavros
34	Moyer's Repair	Janice Rodriguez
40	Historically Inaccurate	Jacob Weber
54	Bone Weight	Shih-Li Kow
68	The Girl You Wanted	Anna Chu
88	Trick Bag	Jane Snyder
104	Carry Me	Patrick Parks
112	The Story Itself	Elizabeth Kirschner
129	Prayer at Such Times	Donna Obeid
131	Local Influencer	Christopher Bell
146	Boy Trouble	Linda Davis
151	This Morning I Woke Up In Another Country	Anthony St. George
161	Cluck	Matt Ingoldby
172	Personalization	Peter Reibling
180	The Urban Gardener Who the Bulbuls Hate	Ash Kaul
184	Born Blue	Robert McGuill
198	Certain Silence	Brett Biebel
204	Art Imitating Life	Thomas Misuraca

Truth

26	Skee-Ball for Grown-Ups	Jim Ross
62	Delinquent	Rowan MacDonald
124	Playing Football for Jesus	Michael Hardin
137	All Heart and No Legs	Katie King
155	I Think I Know Why I Am Afraid	Leah Skay
173	By the Time I Made Oklahoma	C L Hoang
194	The Chase	Charles Jacobson

206   **Contributor Bios**

Dear Precious Reader,

It worked! I hate to admit that I was skeptical. I was convinced that doing away with our reading fee would open us to being carpet-bombed with inferior quality work and submissions that failed to meet our submission guidelines. Although there were a few of those, the real news is the phenomenal quality and diversity, not to mention the sheer volume of submissions we received. Every once in a while, it's redeeming to be wrong. This is the largest and most diverse issue of *The Ocotillo Review* to date. It also features the winners from our 2022 Summer writing contests as well as a few of the short-listed stories from the Chester B. Himes Memorial Fiction Prize. I stand pleasantly rebuked!

I'm right about one prediction though. When we decided to do away with the annual themed issue I stated that each submission call tends to develop a theme organically. It's true for this anthology. As I began reviewing the poems and stories chosen by our editorial staff it became obvious that a significant percentage of the chosen art featured plots and characters who fell outside of societal norms in their familial and cultural interactions. So, this issue is deemed The Alternative Family Issue. Not every piece falls into those parameters but enough do to to call it a theme.

There are so many highlights in this issue it would require several paragraphs to enumerate them, but I'll share a few I feel you shouldn't miss.

The opening poem by M Ann Reed perfectly sets the tone for this compilation.

We rarely choose to publish more than two or three poems by any one poet but the 5 Ghazals by Shannon Mann intertwined on several levels. It would have amounted to sacrilege to remove any of them from the group.

Scott Lowery's prize-winning poem, *Somewhere In America,* "reaches towards a tenuously constructed masculinity with both love and nostalgia for that *'sad song of beer and baseball'*." - Zoë Fay-Stindt, contest judge

If you want prose with a poignant emotional grasp the runner-up for the Himes Fiction Prize, Patrick Parks' *Carry Me* brings the juice, as does Shih-Li Kow's *Bone Weight.*

Looking for wry humour and a happy(?) ending? Matt Ingoldby's *Cluck* should fill the bill.

In our truth column, Katie King's *All Heart and No Legs* suggests how to deal with young love when it goes horribly wrong.

Our last story in this compilation is Thomas Misuraca's *Art Imitating Life.* What is our responsibility as artists? It's a call to action or at least a thought-provoking ending to an outstanding collection.

I suppose as long as we can afford to, we will continue to accept submissions without a reading fee. We do have a "tip jar" and I hope folks who submit or read our journal will support us with a donation. You can also purchase back issues of *The Ocotillo Review* and other titles from our website www.kallistogaiapress.org.

Thank you for your support these past seven years and I hope we can continue to bring you outstanding literary works into the distant future.

Have a lovely 2023.

It could have happened otherwise

It was inevitable, Dad.
It could have happened otherwise, Dad.
But it didn't, Dad.

You were defending a gifted artist's career choice,
though his father, your friend, had threatened to 'disown' him.
You were driving home, pleading your case with Mom,
while I was listening from the backseat, searching
the starry night's incubating possibilities,
finding my golden thread spinning a halo around
my star – the hot blue one – and, likening you
to Shakespeare extolling mercy as true justice
(surely favorable to the artist's aim, yours
and mine) I announced my career choice to be
        a Shakespeare dramaturge.

NO! you exploded, so opposite your Irish-English
reticence, as simultaneously you braked
between city blocks – then fast-forwarded,
tumbling backseat grocery bags to the floor.

"But you supported –" "It's not the same!" you defended,
accelerating home while Mom floored invisible brakes
below the front suicide seat, which often fail to work,

and like Shakespeare's Viola, *all of her father's sons
and all of the daughters, too,* I morphed into your son,
Icarus, expelled out the car window, to try the self-forgetting
wings, yet unfledged, that could fly with beauty –

How blind I had been. Hadn't known your story –
how once you had been a *wandering bark,*
a country boy, *whose worth is unknown although his height
be taken,*
sea-tossed by city-slicker high school boys and bullied
by an English teacher you had nicknamed *Miss Macbeth!*

Your graduation photo depicts a gargoyle's face
suspended to ward off evil from the heights of a cathedral.
-

What had we learned? *How the course of true love
never did run smooth?* You creating beautiful rooms
and Rumi gardens for convalescing patients?

Me, gardening Shakespeare's world of restorative justice?

How kin to Shakespeare you are astonishes me.
The Green World had called you both to tend gardens –
to learn how they teach us to be wise, humble, and
            gardeners of humankind.

- M. Ann Reed

Jean-Martin Charcot (29 November 1825 – 16 August 1893) was a French neurologist and professor of anatomical pathology. He worked on hypnosis and hysteria, and is known as "the founder of modern neurology", and his name has been associated with at least 15 medical eponyms, including various conditions sometimes referred to as Charcot diseases.

—Wikipedia Excerpt

Paris, 1886

Elbow-Length Gloves

My ambivalence toward the renowned neurologist Jean-Martin Charcot took root when I was still the novice transcriber, only recently permitted on the Salpêtrière grounds. I had worked many months assisting at his private practice before granted the honor of the Salpêtrière, having to outlast his persistent admonitions that working in a hospital populated with the disease-ridden and addle-minded required unwavering strength.

Repeatedly he asked, "Can Mademoiselle Forette, each and every day inside the walls of the Salpêtrière, face the torments of the deranged, demented and diseased without succumbing to needless pity?" And always keen to remind me that there was more than enough emotional distress among six thousand abandoned women without adding a pinch more emotion, be it compassion or commiseration.

My response never wavered. "I am at your service, Dr. Charcot, to record the truth."

One day, at last, he concluded with a sigh of resignation. "Yes, Mademoiselle Forette, I do suspect that you have the nerves of steel required."

Thus, my stenographic duties inside the Salpêtrière complex began. On mornings Charcot required my services, I entered through the Mazarin gate, flanked by two massive Egyptian pillars which never failed to set my heart racing, as though I were entering an ancient temple, a temple of science. And my religion was science.

To follow the energetic Charcot through the wards kept one in a breathless state of anticipation. His teaching style continuously fascinated everyone as the doctor found the most novel ways to make his case for a diagnosis. The tours, especially, were constructed with such mastery that I thought of them as works of art.

The 'Elbow Length Gloves' incident occurred on such a tour, a blindingly bright, extremely warm day in June. Charcot had been conducting a rather exhaustive amble through Salpêtrière's maze of streets, extolling to a group of six interns the self-sufficiency of the institution. He showed them the general store, tobacco shop, and café where patients, who were able to work, could spend their earnings. He relished telling the newcomers that Salpêtrière was once a prison. "Erected in the 17th century, at Louis IV's insistence, to house the women of loose and easy virtue, but as you can now see" —His admiring interns, staff and new stenographer following him through the library, the school and the newly converted gymnasium— "all radically changed for the benefit of our Salpêtrière residents."

Outside the wine shop, I recorded what I thought his concluding remarks, "Yes, we even have a wine merchant, but to counterbalance such indulgences," he chuckled, pointing his cane toward the distant St. Louis dome, "a Catholic Church and, for further balance, a Protestant chapel nearby. Now, let us climb to..."

The sentence interrupted, as his assistant Giles de la Tourette silently mouthed the words, *trop de vent*, too much wind. Charcot began to study the poplar trees whose tips were slightly swaying, then up at the sky where quick moving clouds were suddenly covering the sun. He nodded to la Tourette. "But first, let's explore some of our nearby industries."

We entered a building of workshops where women mended sheets, sewed chemises, aprons and nursing bonnets which were largely allocated to other public hospitals in Paris. He explained that work at the Salpêtrière was mandatory for the residents and patients. "As long as they are physically and mentally able. And we give them latitude to choose their hours. They receive payment for their labor, a nominal sum to be sure, as we don't wish them to become extravagant."

He smiled proudly at the workers we passed, many shyly looking up at their Director, clearly happy and nervous with his visit. During the entire walk-through the various workshops both la Tourette and Charcot stole glances out the window, seemingly checking weather conditions.

Unexpectedly the taciturn Tourette cried, "Professor Charcot! The clouds and winds have dispersed! The sun shines! Not a leaf on the poplars stirs!"

Here was a shout of unmistakable joy, la Tourette sticking his head out the window, Charcot rushing to confirm what seemed to them a miraculous turn of good fortune. "My goodness! So, yes, it is quite calm!"

For the two men to view a turnaround in the weather as some miraculously beneficent event seemed quite unusual, yet naively I fell into thinking, What a charming response for such eminent doctors, to be so enthused for the re-emergence of the summer sun.

What I would eventually learn in the hour to follow was that Dr. Charcot took a near childlike delight in orchestrating neurological surprises for his audiences, and one waited for us.

Resuming our outdoor tour, we passed the vegetable gardens and fruit orchards busily tended by Salpêtrière's women residents. One elderly soul, surprisingly agile, ran to Charcot and reverently handed him a fresh peach. Gladly he accepted her gift before giving the peach to Tourette for safekeeping. Charcot seemed eager to continue leading our group upward, climbing a steep rise until at last he stopped before a sweeping view of the Salpêtrière complex.

Leaning upon his cane, he wanted everyone time to absorb the vastness of his domain. "Some call Salpêtrière the shadow city and Paris the city of light. For Jean-Martin Charcot..." he reflected, removing the black chimney hat to daub his forehead with a handkerchief, "the reverse is more accurate. Out there..." he waved his top hat, "in the hundreds of buildings you see, the laboratories, research centers, clinics, in each, we work under a light different than Paris, ours is the torchlight of science which will not, cannot be extinguished."

Charcot's profile transfixed everyone, a strong, handsome countenance having the noble bearing of a Napoleon, a Dante, and sculpted into the face his dedication for all the women living and interred at the Salpêtrière. He took out a small comb from his breast pocket to smooth back his unconventionally long hair and replaced his chimney hat.

Then we descended in an unfamiliar direction, trudging single file down a paved walkway, passing several miniature parks which Charcot noted, "served our more meditative residents." He inexplicably began tapping the paving stones as we walked, as if in secret code to signal someone his approach. When he stopped in front of an ornamental iron gate, we were all perspiring from the sun's heat. He pushed open the gate. "Let us find shade here."

Entering, we took in our surroundings, a green carpeted park abundantly shaded with willow trees, their branches bending heavily with leaves. Charcot had lapsed into puzzling silence, he simply stared at us. It was his most celebrated feature, his penetrating stare, which few were inclined to confront for any length of time. I personally found truth in the talk that if one looked directly into the steel greyness of his eyes, one never forgot them. The group well aware of the doctor's reputation as the supreme hypnotist of Paris grew increasingly uncomfortable under the weight of his demanding gaze. Yet, what was he seemingly waiting for us to comprehend? Each person looked around.

We were not alone.

Deeper into the park, visible through the drooping willows, three women sat on a stone bench in a grassy clearing. A painter could not have conjured a more pleasing image: all three ladies were magnificently dressed in high-necked, white muslin dresses. And despite the day's torrid heat, the women wore white, elbow-length gloves which matched the gorgeous white cream of their dresses. Farther behind them a grey wall, speckled with mildew, served almost as a painted backdrop.

They were like a sitting-room tableau, three genteel women adorned with large, fashionable hats, completely engaged, so it seemed, in an animated discussion, and each of their hats supported one long, feathered plume, the plumes busily waving as they chatted.

Catching Charcot's smile turn sly, I guessed we were in the midst of a planned event. He gave a showman's sweep of the cane to invite us to approach the ladies on the stone bench. No one budged, no one prepared to be the first to advance. Instead, the interns exchanged uncertain glances. Charcot's response was to shrug and walk a short distance away. He took the peach from

Tourette, sat at another bench, and focused on eating, making a grand show of indifference as to what we chose to do.

Eventually, an irresistible urge had the group moving, en masse, slowly toward the women. I joined them, prodded by an almost giddy sense of intrigue.

Let's listen, I said to myself, or eavesdrop on what these elegantly attired women are discussing.

Their feathered plumes continued to happily wave, each dyed a different colour, delicate ostrich feathers, a light blue, a buttery yellow and a red closer to rose.

We drew nearer until their features took form and life. One young intern was unable to stifle a gasp. At close range, the gentility we imagined was replaced by a depiction of infirmity.

Our group, to a person, struggled with disappointment. The three women were a haggard lot. We saw care-worn faces belonging to the Salpêtrière, women who had spent many sorrowed years at the asylum. We had not come upon a tea party, not ladies conversing about art and literature, but Salpêtrière residents uncontrollably shaking with various palsies.

Charcot came behind us. "What you are witnessing are three distinct manifestations of tremors—three discrete neurological maladies." With a quick signal from la Tourette, I moved to the side and began transcribing. "But can anyone of you, my neurologists of the future," Charcot continued with his sly smile, "distinguish one tremor from the other? Can someone here make an accurate diagnosis of each woman's condition? Regard them carefully. Is there, perchance, a measuring device at your disposal?"

Charcot waited. No one ventured a response. The silence lingered unpleasantly. The women, all far into their sixties, maintained their trembling poses, speaking not a word, probably coaxed to show off their fashionable wardrobes. I could not tolerate the growing awkwardness.

"The feather," I spoke up.

Charcot's aide-de-camp shot me a furious look, la Tourette fuming. His thoughts were easy to read: How dare she, a stenographer, a woman, an employee callow to the ways of the Salpêtrière, have the impertinence to actually respond!

Charcot was only amused and curious. "How so, Mademoiselle Forette?"

"The blue feather," I said, certain of my observations as the woman with the pale blue feather expressed a certain elegance in her movements, "exhibits an alternating rhythm, from complete immobility to a sweeping yet rather volatile undulation, a stop-start cycle occurring approximately every thirty seconds."

"Stomp my cane, excellent! What our recordist just described is one of the tremor conditions attributable to multiple sclerosis." He looked for more information. "And what of the woman with the yellow feather?"

I studied her, a petite woman, surely the oldest of the trio. She sat at the far end of the bench, looking absentmindedly in the distance. The heat was taking its toll on her heavily powdered face, dark rivulets of perspiration coursed down yellowish powdered cheeks.

"The yellow feather exhibits a rapid and continuous fluttering."

"Precisely! A distinct feature of Parkinson's disease! But what can one say with regard to our woman with the red feather? I forewarn you, this tremor confounds most students."

Someone, I realized, had crudely attempted to coordinate the colour of the feathers with each woman's make-up. The red-plumed woman, sitting in the middle, a head taller than the others, had her lantern jaw caked with scarlet rouge, it too starting to melt with the heat.

"The red feather flutters rapidly then sometimes subsides," I said.

"Is there a consistent cycle?"

"It appears erratic."

"What!" Charcot's hands spread outward in mock bewilderment. "A disease with no rules?"

"Wait, I see!" (Oh, how caught up I was in the excitement of discovery!) "The fluttering begins only when the woman attempts to move her body. If she makes no attempt at movement the tremor is controlled."

"Superb! Mademoiselle has thrown a light upon our demonstration clearer than that of the noon day sun. Our patient with the red feather actually suffers from the same disease as the patient with the yellow feather, Parkinson's, but it is at a less severe state of degeneration. You are a true observer, Mademoiselle Recordist."

"Our probationary recordist," came la Tourette's sarcastic barb.

Charcot, choosing not to contradict his chief assistant's authority, nodded gravely. "It is a position sorely in need of being filled. Show us your note taking later," he put out his order gruffly. But I knew Charcot, long ago, had made his favorable decision with me.

La Tourette, however, pored over my notes later that afternoon in Charcot's outpatient office while Charcot, secretly amused, kept a respectful distance. La Tourette put on his wire-rims to scrutinize every line. Every word.

After completing his careful review, he gave me a very unhappy look. "Your dictation is without error," he acknowledged curtly. "It is verbatim."

Charcot, for his assistant's benefit, feigned surprise. "Isn't Mademoiselle Forette simply amazing!" The notepad returned, I felt the depth of Charcot's stare, as he never tired of seeking some place behind my thoughts. "Has the lady sent you to me?" he asked.

Lady??

Charcot savored my confusion. "Providence," he smiled.

A question I didn't answer.

At day's end, heading home to Madame Dujardin's boarding house, my steps were light, buoyed by pride. I had shown my ability to observe accurately, proved my competence as a verbatim recordist, and engendered admiration from the world's greatest neurologist. I was elated.

What then, when reaching the door, gave me a vague, unsettled feeling? My self-importance had strangely eroded, replaced by a kind of shakiness, disorientation, something amiss. When I took to re-examining my behavior toward the palsied women, it now seemed reprehensible. My eagerness to participate in Charcot's neurological games and parade my powers of perception came at what cost? Had I not, for a taste of Charcot's approval, made myself a complicit partner in the theatrical demonstration? Surrendering scruples, daring to view the feathered plumed ladies as necessary object lessons. I was disgusted with myself.

In an emotional turmoil, I hurried inside to find Madame Dujardin. Would she please have the porter fill my tub for a bath? The only thought was to immerse myself in water, as hot as I could tolerate, a cleansing of the guilt which clung like dirt. The women of Salpêtrière were not playthings.

Slowly, I slipped into the tub top full with water and, as hoped, so hot it felt almost intolerable. I sank down until the water lapped to my chin. Closing my eyes did not help. The ostrich feathers were fluttering to measure the depths of disease. I remembered the ancient Egyptian belief that when dead souls passed into the underworld, their hearts were weighed on the Scales of Judgment and measured against the single feather of truth. The ibis-headed scribe Thoth recorded the results. If the scales fell into balance, the dead kept their hearts and were guided into the Boat of the Sun, forever blessed, conducted across the waters to a heaven called the Elysian Fields. If measured unworthy, the heart was devoured by a beast—the heartless soul condemned to a netherworld, ruled by chaos.

I submerged and held my breath to rid myself of the day's events, to ward away the women and their trembling feathers. When my lungs wanted to burst, I shot up, gasping for air, only to see the three palsied women, side by side under the fierce, noon-day sun. Three kindly women coerced to wear elbow-length gloves, abiding the fate of sweltering heat, the different coloured rouges melting in rivulets down their aged faces. The gloves they wore, white cotton, high-buttoned, in the almost unbearable heat, their elbow-length gloves.

- R.w. Meeks

Heritage

I inherited my father's nose (who inherited his father's righteousness and his mother's color blindness) and my mother's hostility (who inherited her mother's hospitality and her father's nervous smile). My father's father inherited his father's aura migraines (who inherited his father's high cholesterol and his mother's manner of eating without chewing) and his mother's hair (who inherited her mother's falsetto and her father's tempo). My father's mother inherited her mother's elation (who inherited her father's empathy and her mother's diabetes) and her father's sweat glands (who inherited his father's alcoholism and mother's silence). My mother's mother inherited her father's introversion (who inherited his father's laugh lines and his mother's poor memory) and her mother's fingernails (who inherited her mother's moustache and father's metabolism). My mother's father inherited his father's insomnia (who inherited his father's potbelly and his mother's eye dust) and his mother's baldness (who inherited her mother's freckles and her father's sweet tooth). We may as well be born as mirrors.

- Karan Kapoor

sleep: fragments

since he refuses to speak
I observe him sleep
the whole experience is akin
to crossing an ocean
walking on a bridge made of stones
except it's not stones it's electricity
and the ocean's not an ocean
but your father's soul

*

a ten-inch mattress
rests on the floor
(*the bed to far*
off the ground for me)
beside my mother's diwan

uneasy as time   he moves
from one side to another
ever vhanging
his position like Jupiter

one could be so restless
only in a body
they want   to escape

*

My voice is your voice
my empty chair your empty chair
my budding bald spot your bald head
my wakeful sleep your wakeful sleep

*

what if all these poems about him
are like a movie which loses everything
good about the book

*

the Jupiter of his body   collides
with the diwan

*

one afternoon I inform him he hums in his sleep

there is no one who does not
some bable   others sing gospel

*

perhaps if we said *Please*
Please Rain   Please Tuesday
please sleep

*

no alcoholic steps into the same sleep twice

*

is a poem beginning
          their was a time my father
or a poem fashioned from his insomnia
          a portrait of the father or the poet
                    or both or neither

*

so glad your snores are solely yours

*

night   an orshestra of insects
sleep   an abandoned hall

*

you've got to be a ceiling fan to understand any of this

*

all dreams   memory after waking
all words   law after believing

*

11

the body bleeds out the nights undoing:
here we are again, awake he says to himself, *alive.*

- Karan Kapoor

aubade

love
a hummingbird

the stain of sky
you're rubbing with rags

the dome of moon
when cut neat in half

the bass of his laugh
rain cleansing a river

the river giving itself
back to the sky

the smell of dandelion
wine he ages

love travels sitting
on the shoulders of light

love is light's
unspoken ache

coyotes do not have a word for love
coyotes howl

all night lovers ask do you love me
all night the manifold beloveds howl

years ago a teacher asked us to sew a flag
for a country called Love my father carried me

to the terrace & pointed upwards
let's scissor a piece of sky

so your flag is full of stars

- Karan Kapoor

Try Harder

Stop thanking me. I am not your servant

I want to kiss you frankly
with a star at your crown
risk swollen and leaking

I peel on the logic romper: still sporting
these white kiddie eyelets
The little sputtered lions glint dumbly

What is the shape of my desire
What is its banner, its direction
What is its flamethrower. What are its shoes

my obdurate foolishness   or just my failure of imagination

I tried to write a history of my early depravity
but my sister says try harder   it's not depraved at all

There's a really high turnover rate for these characters
$10 an hour inside a very hot costume

They give you a free mug that you can fill
with whatever bottomless sugar

Can strategy exist in a loving way
or is it a zero-sum game

Why did my bank pick this gringo
to speak its automated options system
even in Spanish. Por favor marque ocho

I don't want to be blessed
I want to be eaten

I still regret not letting Sonja paint me naked

- Jennifer MacKenzie

Sensus Fidelium

The argument about holiness gets hotter
in the presence of distinct shittiness, or evil

Is there anyone who didn't think Tiki bars were racist

I can fix my eyes on B's face and still monitor your breathing
the rise and fall of your breasts inside your sweater

Is it faster. Are you feeling the presence of my body too

I don't mind if all the saints look on while I kiss you
Can they read my mind that I want to kiss you

at your dinner table meditating on the possible
masculinity of dark wool. Terse but sensual too

I would hope they don't mind
I would hope they bless us

and eclipse any primness in us
with thanks and candor

I want to eat your welcome blurred
or clear with my chipped grin

To unfurl in your burred tenderness
clenched unadorned, unpleating

I memorize the line of campfire ash
under your short square nails

You say you didn't know the Arabs
brought Aristotle to Europe

What Bruno needed to not be burned
in Rome's Campo di Fiori was zero

In America you dodge polite pity
for being a poet. By you I mean me

I mean there is no calculus without zero
This giant machine was not designed
to perceive what it's crushing

- Jennifer MacKenzie

Caring for Her

Standing **by the window, she thinks: what is a liana?** A name? She'll ask him that. He knows everything. Any problem, any doubt, she asks him. She sends her questions to his mind, and the answers come back to her as if they are her own answers coming from her mind. But they're not. They're imprints. The palimpsest of her own mind hovers somewhere below and rarely surfaces. When it does, it has no answers, but many colours.

And also, what is a triothorpe? This is a word she's seen or heard or read in an almanac. She'll ask him that too.

She's leaning on the window, palms pressed against the glass, looking out. The driveway, newly tarred, looks like the back of a sleek sleeping sea monster, with impatiens clustered along the edge, like roaming cuttle fish. But what is a cuttle fish? She planted those flowers, with his help. Or was it – he planted them with hers? She held the little plastic pots. He dug. He planted. Last spring. They lie now – not like fish – but like a pattern of bright coins beside the flat black tar top – or they are tiny moons catching the light of the rising sun. Jupiter has six.

He is asleep in the room next to hers. She'll wake him up and ask: liana, triothorpe. She'll ask the exact spelling. It is: L-I-A-N-A. It is: T-R-I-O-T-H-O-R-P-E.

She draws the curtains aside and watches the sun rise. Bleary eye of the universe, half asleep. He loves the universe. Tells her stories about it: how time is the same in all parts of it, how it breathes like a cat. How it is alive like sparks of fire. Why is he still asleep? Why can't he be awake when she is awake? He never is.

Too early to make coffee. A new yawn of light opens up in a rift of cloud. The sky is waking up.

She shakes her fists, presses them against her temples, against the window. How will his answer go? It will be: A liana is… A triothorpe is… And the universe is expanding at a rate of. And you can't eat cuttle fish. Or you can. But he's been asleep for so long! Years now, years. All the years. Forty-two for him, and fifty-three for her. Birthday next June. Maybe he will take her to Burger King for a cheeseburger and onion rings. Three slices of pickle. Only a few minutes now. Five to five-fifteen, five-fifteen to five-thirty. Many minutes plus many minutes. A comet's tail of long, stretching minutes until she can wake him up.

Stringiness of nerves standing here waiting. Too early to go into his room. He'll get mad and shout. And she hasn't made any coffee yet.

Outside, joggers are running in the dawn light. Red shirts, yellow shorts. All in the same colors, a team. White shoes, white as seagulls.

She must show him this – the strangeness of these joggers so early! The strangeness of that branch reaching up into the sky, a skeleton hand asking the sky for an answer.

Wake up! Fifteen minutes and she'll go in. Can't wait. After five long minutes, she creeps down the hall in her blue flannel nightgown, knocks lightly on his door, then scratches it, then opens it and tiptoes in. She lifts a chair and nudges it over beside his bed. Sits.

He's asleep, his mouth slightly open, head turned to one side.

"What is a liana?"

He is dead asleep, still as stone, still as the corpse of their father.

"What is a triothorpe? Do you know what that is? You must know."

He turns now, blinks his eyes open and stretches. Pulls a sheet up over his head and pulls it back down. Yawns. Coughs.

"A liana is a creeping vine," he says and coughs again. "What time is it?"

"Ten o'clock."

"No it's not."

"It's nearly ten."

He leans over and checks his phone. "It's five twenty-seven." He sighs and falls back into the bed. "Did you make coffee yet?"

"No, it's too early to make coffee."

"You may as well make it now. Three scoops and a full pot, not boiling."

"Why is a liana the name of a creeping vine? Because I thought it was an animal."

"It's not."

"It could be."

"But it's not." He pulls a pillow over his head.

"And a triothorpe?" She lifts a corner of the pillow and leans in close to his face, her right eye next to his.

"I have no idea what that is. I never heard of it. Please. Can you –"

"I think it's a kind of a weapon. Knights carried them on horseback. They rode into battle, brandishing their triothorpes against the universe."

"Can I sleep for twenty more minutes – please?"

"I need to know now."

"I don't know."

"But you know everything."

"I know things that exist, not things that don't." He curls into a small ball under the covers. She lifts the edge and peeks in, then leans over close until her nose is on the pillow, almost touching his.

"Make me a coffee. I'll tell you then," he says.

"And a quill?"

"You know what a quill is. It's a pen made with a feather."

"Uh huh." She stands up and looks down at him. "I'll make the coffee now."

"Good," he says from under the covers.

"And why would someone want to write with a feather?"

No answer. He has fallen asleep. She shuffles out of the room.

In the moment before he loses consciousness, he sees an image of her pouring a whole bag of coffee beans into his suitcase and adding water, then lighting a fire under the suitcase. He sits up, looks round. "Where are you?" he says. "What are you doing?"

He gets out of bed and bolts downstairs.

It's going to be a long day. A long life.

- Rosalind Goldsmith

Looking to the Stars

Astronauts watch this city blaze
from space. It twinkles, a star itself.
Every brick column mailbox here
sits exactly twelve inches from the curb,
every lawn mowed two inches high.
Run-off glitters the gutter,
copious water for non-indigenous shrubs.
I sit for a friend's dog, walk her
up Black Oak, down Burwood,
homes lighted like the panel of a 747.
This piece of Dallas juts into suburbia,
wedged between Carrollton and Plano.
My friend, more factual than tactful,
says I can park in back if I wish,
but even curbside I won't be suspect –
I drive the same car as his maid.
Perhaps it's my upbringing –
there's much I'll never understand –
but I just can't see the stars from here.

- Ann Howells

On an Evening Walk by the Texas State
Lunatic Asylum Cemetery

This is the place where the road shifts its hips,
where the pastel bungalows' crooked porches behold a chain link fence
that imprisons eleven green acres and a few dozen headstones.
They emerge through dusk dust in the color *bone,*
piercing the wet living world as if teething into gums of grass.

This is the place where three-thousand souls and a row of remains
rest; where state staff once marked the bodies of Pearl, Arthur, Rene,
Eva, with numbered wooden sticks; where *lunatic* came from
lunatique, came from *luna,* came from *moon-struck*—
This is the place where the pace slows and the breath

deepens in the belly; where stillness warns the attentive
reader that the mind can be an deceptive place, like a flat
field in the moonlight freckled with a few dozen phrases,
while thousands of voices sing sorrows out of sight.

- Greta Rasmus

Amor Mortis

At this age, so much nearer the end,
       I don't want to kill anything.
The tiny green bug that traverses
       my notebook gets a reprieve, but
even that puts me into a place of phony
       superiority, as if I'm a god who decides.

There's a rat in our backyard.
       I called the Orkin man who
put out poison in locked containers.
       My neighbor said he found a dead rat
in his backyard. So here I am, a wager
       of chemical warfare at 72.

I refused to kill people who hadn't
       done anything to me during Vietnam.
Now, after a lifetime of pacifism,
       there are people I believe who could
benefit from a bullet, who should be
       removed from the human stream.

Is this our impossible nature?
       The violence of kindness?
The kindness of some violence?
       Does our path of love crossroad
with a deadly determination, a self-
       destructive drive toward extinction?

Everything I've killed in my life—
       insects, fish, rabbits, and rats—
have taken a part of me with them
       into nothingness and caused,
at my core, a profound
       disappointment with myself.

- Charles Brice

Spin

I'm here today, as I am every day,
ensconced in my third-floor study
writing poems. I've been here like
this for three years now. I prefer

to think of it as a staycation—a time
out of time while still firmly embedded
in time. It's like I've gone somewhere,
travelled to a land called Poetry, but

never had to leave anywhere. It's like
running in place: you huff and wheeze,
maybe even threadbare a swath of carpet,
but the scenery never changes—

no challenging hills or cheering crowds.
Still, you can say that you've had a run.
This is what is called "spin" these days,
itself a staycation for language since,

when you spin something, nothing turns.

- Charles Brice

Dreams

Sadie says she can't remember her dreams.

"What do you think that means?" she asks me, a wrinkle of concern creasing her forehead beneath wisps of auburn hair.

It's Saturday morning, and Sadie and I are having a lazy breakfast at home because for once I don't have to rush off to be somewhere, and it feels good, and it's a relief, and I can breathe, and I want to spend more time like this with Sadie since I don't feel I see her enough during the week. My contribution to our meal is scrambled eggs with spinach and red onion and green peppers and shredded cheddar cheese and chunks of the salty country ham we bought at the farmers' market, along with slices of toast, and Sadie made pumpkin pancakes on the electric griddle we got from her parents last Christmas that I still can't understand how to properly use and I probably never will.

I tell Sadie that I don't know, and I don't know, and truth be told I can't remember my dreams either. I just sleep, and then I wake, and I go about my day, which has been perfectly fine with me, or at least it hasn't bothered me, hasn't seemed out of the ordinary or caused me concern, not until Sadie brings this up and now it gets me thinking about it too, though I suppose not as much as Sadie, what with how she gets.

"I used to *love* my dreams," Sadie says as she cuts a piece of pancake with the side of her fork and scoots it through the puddle of maple syrup on her plate before raising it to her face, as if to get a better look, and a sniff, and then gliding it into her mouth. "They were so vivid, so clear." She swallows. "It was almost a letdown to have to get up." Sadie hesitates, and sighs, and moves a hand through her hair, pushing it out of her face, to no avail. "Which is wrong, I know." Another sigh. "Now, as soon as I open my eyes, the dreams drift away, flutter from my grasp, just out of reach … and gone." Sadie shakes her head. "I don't get it."

"Could be that you like your waking life better," I say, and I try to come across as confident, as I douse my eggs with hot sauce and shovel them into my mouth. I gulp them down, so I can complete my thought. "Remember how unhappy you were—" I stop myself, and I stutter, "what with … everything." I consider how best to put it. "But now, you're better," I say, and then I swiftly correct course, "you're happier. You're happy." To truly recover, though it might be too late, I say, like I'm some expert on the subject, "So you don't need your dreams anymore." After a moment, doing my best to be subtle, I say, "You *are* happy?" I swallow. And, my voice lower now, "That guy, that … doctor—he's helping you?"

There's a lull that lasts just a few seconds but seems longer before Sadie says, "mm-hmm," and, "uh-huh," drawn out and fading like she wasn't really listening but rather that she's contemplating, lost within herself, her brow furrowed, staring intently at the remains of the eggs on her plate, driving the corner of a piece of dried toast through them, not to eat, just to do. "Even so," she glances up at me—those blue eyes, "I'd like to remember *some* of my dreams."

"Maybe you will," I say, and I realize how dismissive that comes across as soon as I say it but I can't take it back so I just act like I meant it sincerely, and I did. "You know?"

Sadie and I continue eating, in silence, with the only sound that of the stoic clock on the wall someone gave us as a wedding gift that I wish we would have taken back ticking in a foreboding cadence. I scramble to think of what else to say, a change in subject preferably, to fill this void, but Sadie beats me to it.

"What if I *never* remember my dreams again?" Sadie asks, nearly pleads. "What a sorry state that will be."

"You'll …" I begin, not sure where I'm going but with the need to jump in all the same. "You'll remember your dreams again. Your brain is just filtering out which dreams are worth remembering."

I wait, to see if that resonates with Sadie, and it actually resonates with me, surprisingly, and I briefly impress myself that I could be on to something.

"Yeah," Sadie concedes, and she shrugs, and she returns to her plate. "That could be it."

"Of course it is," I say confidently, perhaps too confidently but I'm full of myself at this instant because it does make sense.

Sadie and I continue to eat.

"Good job on the eggs, buddy," Sadie says, wrangling what's left of the scrambled eggs on her plate with her fork, using her piece of toast as a guide, and unapologetically cramming it all into her mouth for an overstuffed bite. "This is *definitely* your thing," she mumbles, then swallows and wipes her lips—those lips—with her napkin. "Your scrambled eggs kick ass!"

"Your pancakes kick ass," I say, not as enthusiastic but that's just me. "You've mastered the fine art of the griddle."

"Someday I might teach you how to use it," Sadie says, a sly grin, and she's back to being her, and she's back to me, and I can breathe. "But for now, let's just leave this as my thing."

I tell Sadie that that's fine with me, and it is, and we finish our breakfast, and we clear the table, and we put our dishes in the sink, and we go about our day, to enjoy the rest of the weekend together, with no more talk about dreams.

- Peter Stavros

25

Skee-Ball for Grownups

I'm in the passenger seat trying to disentangle a Slinky that my grandson Ben, age 7, had been doing magic tricks with. I assured him I was an expert at this. Evidently, I lied. It's getting more inextricably tangled by the moment. I want to hit backspace to return Ben's Slinky to the condition in which he entrusted it to me. I want to snip out the muddle in the middle and fuse the two ends together. Even if I could, the remainder would be so short it could barely make it down a single step in a dollhouse.

Ben is sitting directly behind me so he can't see the mess I've made of this. I slip the Slinky under my seat to hide it, not from him, but from me. Tempted again and again, I keep slipping it out from under to see if perhaps it's been magically repaired.

As we pass the turnoff for Atlantic City, I say, "There was a time when Atlantic City's grand old hotels lined the boardwalk. Mr. Peanut walked along the boardwalk to lead people to the Mr. Peanut shop. Hawkers tried to entice walkers to come see their new wonder product—a shampoo that makes your hair shine, a stain remover that leaves no trace of spilled red wine, an all-in-one screwdriver—at pop-up stores scattered along the boardwalk."

My daughter/Ben's mother, who is at the wheel, says, "Tell Ben about the Flying Horses."

"Hey Ben," I say, "You been listening?"

"To what you said about Mr. Peanut?"

"Just checking. Mommy wanted me to tell you about Steel Pier."

"What about it?"

"When I was a kid, top acts—really famous people—came there to perform. At the end of the pier there was a high diving board. Horses dove off the diving board—people claimed the horses flew through the air—as they dove into the ocean."

"Why didn't the horses get killed?"

"There was always a rider who kept them safe."

"How come they both didn't get killed?"

"I don't know. Maybe they did. They stopped diving when I was a kid."

"How come we've never gone to Atlantic City?"

"Atlantic City got old," I say. "The hotels got run down. People stopped going there. Somebody bought them up and tore them all down."

"Why didn't they fix them?"

"They thought they had a better idea. In their place, they built casinos."

"Casinos are a big scam," says Ben. "You can't win. The casinos make you think you can, but that's all an illusion. It's like Skee-Ball for grownups.

Who would do that?"

"Donald Trump would. As part of his quote real estate empire un-quote, he built all these supposedly fancy modern hotels to convince people to bring their money bags to his casinos."

"And leave their bags of money there," says Ben. "Donald Trump is the biggest scammer. We need to put Trump and his minions in prison for life."

"He'd probably just run scams inside of prison," I laugh. "And the prison guards will all be working for him."

"Scams are everywhere," says Ben. "My other grandma keeps falling in love with scammers she meets online. Every time, she thinks they really love her and want to spend the rest of their lives with her. Then, every time, they ask her to send an Apple gift card. She finally realizes it's just another scam. She doesn't send the gift card and soon they stop bothering her. So far, she's been scammed and fallen in love eight times. Every time, she gets sad until another scammer says he loves her and she believes him."

"We get calls from scammers every day," I say. "Several times a day!"

"What's their scam?"

"Ha, different things," I say. "They want to confirm you just spent nine hundred dollars on Amazon and if not, press one and give us your credit card number so we can refund your money."

"How could anybody fall for that?" Ben asks.

"People do. Or your car warranty is expiring and they'll extend it for half price. Or, as part of your health insurance, they want to offer you new benefits for your diabetes, for the pains you have in your back, knees, elbows, wrists. Whatever pains you have, they've got it covered."

"How can people fall for that?"

"I guess, when you're in pain, you get desperate."

"What do you and Grammy do about all these scammers?"

"We've started having fun with the ones calling about health benefits."

"How're you doing that?"

"We've started turning the tables on them. Grammy asks them ques-tions about their own health benefits. I ask them what sorts of pains they have. One caller at a time, they can't hide behind the illusion."

"Do scammers try to get old people to go to casinos too?"

"I know they used to. They'd offer free bus rides to the casinos. Peo-ple would party on the way there but at the end of the day, after they'd thrown away their money, they'd all sit outside, quiet, expressionless, wishing the day would end. I've seen their sad faces."

"I want to stop scammers and scamming," says Ben. "I like how you're scamming the scammers."

"What's your plan? How're you planning to stop them?"

"I'm trying to learn hacking from YouTube. I'm already on the sixth video. If I can hack the scammers, I can stop their scams."

"So you're scamming the scammers too?"

"Not yet," Ben says, "I need to learn how from you and Grammy first. How're you doing with my Slinky?"

"Oh, it's coming along just the way you'd imagine. I think I might send it to Amazon to show them the kind of job I've done."

"Can I see it?" Ben laughs.

"Not yet," I say. "It has to go to Amazon first. Amazon will send your Slinky to you."

"Grandpa, I have a question. Have you watched the YouTube video yet on how to untangle a Slinky?"

- Jim Ross

Appreciate Worms

Even those crawling around the grass
of your gut—even those flesh-rings
on your shoulder blades are jewelry.
The corpses know how behind the veil
of dust and ash, where diamond turns
to salt and sand, there will still be worms
waving at you like flowers praising thunder.

Today I plucked one from the dirt
and watched it squirm in my palm,
so desperate to burrow back home
it mistakes my fingers for soil.
This is the beautiful error of time,
my friend, you are but a few years early.

- Cassady O'Reilly-Hahn

Moyer's Repair

The Maxahocken was high and muddy, rushing like the whirlwind that took Elijah up into heaven and bearing branches that tangled under the center of the Maple Street Bridge, the place where everyone in town knew that Mrs. Elwood C. Moyer had jumped to her death on June 13, 1948. Except, of course, that everyone was wrong.

Ruby walked over the bridge, lunch pail in hand, all of school behind her but graduation day. Her footsteps were hollow on the damp wooden decking, and she stopped in the middle and stared into the churning waters, the place where two years earlier, her mama had stopped and stared. And maybe Ruby was thinking about her mama, but maybe she was just waiting for her brother, Woody, who had always been kind of poky. She opened her pail and pulled a couple of oatmeal cookies from it, one for her and one for Woody.

She had been in charge of the kitchen since one week after her mama was gone. Elwood had tried, but the poor man couldn't cook a lick. That first supper on their own, he had added a can of beans to the leftover stew he found in the icebox and reheated the whole mess. The next day he added a can of Spam to the pot, and the next day a can of tomatoes, followed by a can of corn. That Friday, he added a tin of cinnamon, which made the whole street reek to kingdom come. Even Boise, who was part beagle and part Lord knew what, and Fourteen, all gangly, ravenous mutt, wouldn't eat it.

Chastened, Elwood retreated to what he knew best, peanut butter and jelly sandwiches one day, bologna and mustard the next. After two weeks of sandwiches, Ruby had put herself in charge of cooking, and she always did a first-rate job. Standing now in the middle of the bridge on the last day of school, she squinched one eye at the cookies she had just taken from her pail, frowning a little at how much they had spread on the baking sheet. This was a version of a recipe that Betty Crocker had shared on the radio last winter, and Ruby had been overhauling it so it would be easy enough for even a boy or a man to make, and she had a notebook with recipes just as simple. She smoothed and folded the square of waxed paper the cookies were in. Right about then, Woody caught up to her, a dreamy look on his face.

"Your heavenly Father has a plan for you, Ruby," he said, taking the cookie she offered him. Now if Woody had always had his head in the clouds and rattled on about birds or cars or monsters that lived down by the creek, people would have been sure he was feeble-minded. But he talked about God, which caught them up in wonder and shut their mouths.

"My earthly father has a plan for me." Ruby shaded her eyes against the rays of sun that, after nearly a week of rain, were pushing through clouds. "That plan is to have meatloaf on the table by the time he closes up the shop. You're helping."

"Am I cooking Ruby's Easy Meatloaf again while you lounge around?"

"Yes, you are. But I won't be lounging. I'll be hemming those pants down as soon as you get home and take them off. I've got a surprise for you— today you'll be adding a special glaze to the meatloaf."

"You're going places, Ruby," he said, and she laughed and tugged his arm and started them walking.

Woody dug in his heels when she turned by a stump at the side of the road. "Not Aunt Peaches' place," he said. "I'm not going in there."

He sat on the stump and waited, which is what an upright young man like him ought to do. Aunt Peaches wasn't Ruby and Woody's aunt or anyone else's, and she was no one's wife but more than one man's girl. She had calloused hands and grubby fingernails from keeping the motor of her old Nash alive. "Don't need no man for that," she'd say. Elwood had always considered her a terrible influence on his wife.

Ruby dropped in at Peaches' tar-paper shack at least twice a month and, more often than not, returned clutching a postcard that she hid where her papa wouldn't find it, in a cigar box under a pried-up board on the second-story back porch of her house.

On this very last day of school, Peaches gave Ruby a postcard of the Grand Crystal Tea Room at Wanamaker's in Philadelphia. And while the picture made Ruby smile, the words on the back made her sad:

Only enough money for two years for one of you. So sorry. Will keep plugging away.

Love and such,

Mama

Woody was finished with his cookie, looking hungry, and threatening another growth spurt when Ruby said goodbye to Peaches and started up toward the stump. Her brother gave her an accusing look and quoted, "For nothing is secret, that shall not be made manifest; neither any thing hid, that shall not be known and come abroad. Luke 8:17-19, Ruby."

"Don't look at me like that."

"We reap what we sow, Ruby."

"Well, I reaped a postcard from Mama. Let's go home."

Home was the corner of a row of brick houses, with *Moyer's Repair* on signs in both plate glass windows. On the stoop teetered a sandwich board with a cheery welcome that Ruby had painted; Elwood was good with tinkering but not with people.

It had been quite a surprise in Huffstown that Elwood ever married at all. He came back from the Great War shell-shocked and even shyer than he had been as a boy and spent several years taking gizmos apart and putting them back together in his late father's shop. His Uncle Clovis eventually found him a job as a milkman, which got him out and about and in the sights of Inez, and he was married on the far side of thirty and a father soon after.

They were as happy as most couples, with give-and-take and tussles and making up. But then the second war came—or maybe the old one just came back. Elwood tried to enlist, but it's the darnedest thing, because every Saturday when he went to the firehouse where the recruiter was, they'd take his blood pressure, and it'd shoot way up, and they'd send him away. After a couple of months of this, they thanked him for coming but told him to stay home, that he had done his job in the Ardennes. Inez and Peaches got jobs making parachute cord at the mill down near Reading once the able-bodied boys had gone away, and there were more tussles and less making up in the house on the corner after that. When Elwood and Inez fought, young Ruby would take her brother, the one-eyed cat, and Fourteen and Boise out into the yard where they'd play school, writing on the shed wall with a piece of chalk and lobbing softball questions to the dogs like, "What's seven and seven?" and "What's the capital of Idaho?" The cat usually went AWOL before Ruby called recess.

When the war was over, Inez wanted to keep working, in Reading if she had her way. It was, she said, a far sight better than staying in Huffstown, which had always been too small a place for her. She wanted to squirrel away her earnings in a fund for Ruby and Woody, for she got it into her head that they were college material, and she bragged about them to everyone in town who would stand still long enough to listen. Woody was plenty bright, making all As and with not just one Bible memory verse but somewhere around fifty, but a girl? And Inez would nod and say yes, indeed, that Ruby made all As, too, and would be a fine home economics teacher.

Over the supper table one night, Inez brought it up with Elwood.

"What in thunderation is home economics?" Elwood demanded. "Why would anybody need to go to college to study what she's got at home?"

"She'd learn to teach and to understand chemistry and nutrition and such," Inez said.

"She already cooks fine. I haven't the money for such horsefeathers." He pointed his gravy-covered fork at Ruby and said, "Missy, if you want to be home economical, you do it right here."

Elwood accused Inez of being too high and mighty, a phrase that Woody, off in never-never land, mistook for "high and muddy," and so after supper, Ruby chalked both expressions on the shed wall for him and the dogs and the cat to learn.

After the children's bedtime that night, Elwood accused Inez of being too big for her britches. They might just have called each other names that aren't fit to repeat. It's hard to tell, because these old row homes are sturdy, and even with an ear snugged up to the wall, it's not easy to make out every word from the other side. But the long and the short of it is that Inez wanted something different than she did before the war for both herself and her children, and Elwood had a hard time understanding that.

He was sure the restlessness and lack of common sense was in her blood, and it was plainly in their daughter's, too, because even after Inez was gone, Ruby kept talking about studying home economics. She lifted up Fourteen's silky brown ear to whisper to him that she wanted to join the ranks of Miss Crocker's glamorous kitchen test cooks or one day teach people how to make splendid dinners with electrical appliances—maybe over the television, which, Aunt Peaches promised her, was the wave of the future. Once she had a job, she'd buy her papa a shop somewhere where the broadcast signals reached and he'd add television sets to the things he tinkered with, and she'd get her mama back together with him, and she'd donate enough money to buy a pipe organ in the church that Woody would be the pastor of.

But the postcard with the Grand Crystal Tea Room that Ruby picked up at Aunt Peaches' place had put the kibosh on all those dreams. She frowned as she walked Woody back home. She stopped him when they reached the stoop, and, so soft as to almost be impossible to hear, asked, "Don't you want to know what's in Mama's postcard?"

"Why doesn't she write regular letters to us here at home?" Woody asked for the hundredth time.

"So Papa can't find her and bring her back."

"You think he wants to?"

"Deep down, yes."

Woody didn't have a single verse of Scripture in response.

Ruby said, "She hasn't got enough money to pay for both of us to go to college. I want you to go instead of me. I'll get a job at Yoder's. By the time you finish high school, between Mama and me, we might have enough."

Before Woody could say anything else, Elwood came outside and called them into the parlor. Reverend Zerby was there, as he had been the second Friday of every month since Inez's scarf was found on the muddy bank of the Maxahocken and the river patrol came up from Reading and dragged all the way down to the Schuylkill without finding her. If he ever wondered, like the rest of the town did, how long Elwood would wait to have her declared dead and hold a proper funeral, he didn't let on.

Clearly Elwood was not going to spend what little money he had planting an empty coffin in the ground. Inez was not worthy of the pretense, having packed her suitcase and made her farewells to him and the children in the middle of the night two years before. He never wondered if they'd find her body in the river, because he had enough sense to know that no one packs a bag to do themselves in. And no one talks about their big dream to find a job in Philadelphia and put the children through college and then drowns that dream before they even get out of town. No, he was sure she'd walked to the bridge with Ruby tagging along behind her like a puppy, kissed the girl one last time, and crossed over to the other side in Peaches' Nash to coast down the hill and away from him.

Elwood and Ruby and Woody knew there would never be a funeral. But Reverend Zerby didn't, and he sat in their parlor, turning an envelope end to end in his soft hands.

"Would you like some coffee a while, Reverend?" Ruby asked.

He wouldn't; what he wanted was to share the contents of the letter in that envelope. He cleared his throat and explained that he'd taken the liberty of contacting the dean of his alma mater and the regional synod on Woody's behalf.

"Provided you keep that straight-A average in your senior year and promise to follow college with seminary," Reverend Zerby said, "you'll have a full scholarship to both. And Elwood, this isn't charity. It's Divine Providence, so don't get your dander up."

Elwood swallowed his pride and invited the reverend to stay for supper. Woody prepared an excellent easy meatloaf with a respectable glaze. The reverend said a rambling grace over the meal and left when he was done his coffee and cookies. Afterwards, Ruby's hands trembled as she let out the hem on Woody's pants on the second-floor back porch. She kept stopping and staring off into sky, pondering how Woody's good fortune would change the path of her life.

That night she packed some clothes in a duffel bag, tucking in her mama's postcards, and wrote her papa a note. She nudged Woody awake after eleven and gave him her notebook of easy recipes, tied up with a red ribbon. He walked outside with her, down the street and to the stump by the side of the road, waiting while Ruby knocked on the door of the shack. Ten minutes later, Peaches, yawning, jangled her keys, pulled on a sweater, and told Ruby to put her duffel in the Nash.

Woody hugged Ruby goodbye under a moon like God's thumbnail in the sky. She waved back at him when they started away, her little sobs muffled by the car's engine. But Peaches stopped on the bridge and pointed with her chin at the rearview mirror. Woody ran to the door and yanked it open, and Ruby got out and hugged him one last time, as hard as she had hugged her mama that night when the breeze came and snatched her mama's scarf away. She kissed away the tears on both of his cheeks and told him to study hard and to take care of their papa. Then she took her own scarf and tossed it into the stretched-out branches of a young birch.

Elwood would know what to say to everyone: "It was in her blood." That's what he'd say.

- Janice Rodriguez

The Intersection

A meetup
imagined
in Calabasas
if Phil's house
next door is
available to prevent
a two-year build
nails in tires, noise.
Another car shoots
in, another swishes
the other way
hooked to it
the gas bill
the barbecue
anniversary
a lost friend
my sins
daybreak
big truck

- Lawrence Bridges

The Spitting Wind

The spitting wind blows creeks through the yard as
clouds drown out dawn. A wreath of numbness
hangs on the door of our house as I review mistakes
during the rain, in the wrong town. Time caused
waiting not increase. You are known and unknown.

- Lawrence Bridges

More Than us, but Less than Wind
from a line by--Carmen Giménez Smith

The times when I cannot
Meet you halfway, we struggle
you know how to say this word,
migration, immigration, destiny.
The scattering of people, traveling
away from where they were born,
from war, violence, famine, poverty,
disease. The diaspora stretches out
like a fishing net, across the Mexico
Border and California, Texas, Arizona.
Dragging culture across grassy fields,
dragging language around like a knapsack,
emptying familiar phrases as if they
were bread crumbs along the way.
 How much can we carry? What do we
leave or stay. How much of ourselves
do we remain within our leaving hearts,
the gateway to our lives, our rabbit's foot,
the pelt worn down to bone and dried blood
under the rabbit's clear nail that we finger
in our nearly closed fist when we are scared
and press down so it cuts us wide open.

-Millicent Borges Accardi

Whoever you are

I can only say your name aloud in a machine room
With the same silver breath I exhale smoke at a fan.
O the tremolo chop & choke; a haze-scatter trill now looms.

I name this my mantra, but what I tell you is more in tune
With the sentiments of time's most mediocre conman:
Sir, I can only say your name aloud in a machine room.

Crown me Mammon & you'll see how a king consumes.
Here for a cut; in on the action; or it's goodbye, guilty lamb.
O the tremolo chop & choke; a haze-scatter trill now looms.

Suppose I can stand to clear my throat, grab a guitar & croon:
No one recovers, it is never over, closure is a sham.
But I can only say your name aloud in a machine room.

Suppose I do spend life decorating the inside of my tomb
& that sour luxury of selection turns me out Ayn Rand.
O the tremolo chop & choke; a haze-scatter trill now looms.

Truth: I cannot defend, define, or pronounce this plume.
I bruise by the bone-white tension of interlocked hands.
So, I will only say your name aloud in a machine room,
O my tremolo chop & choke; the haze-scatter trill who looms.

- T.K. Edmond

Historically Inaccurate

As if relationships weren't already hard enough for Olaniyi, she'd gone and made her new one more difficult by telling her best friend Roberta that her boyfriend Jack was a luthier. That can mean a person who makes any kind of stringed instrument, but in Jack's case, he actually made lutes. He made them in his basement, where he stretched thin strips of wood over a foam core. He played the lute, too, at Renaissance festivals, which was where Olaniyi had met him in August.

Her friend Roberta had a theory about men who played unusual instruments. They were Betas, second-fiddle men. They knew, deep-down, they were not evolution's top choice for passing along genes. In order to find status of some sort, they were forced to take up idiosyncratic hobbies like the banjo or juggling. Other suspect men included those who spoke Klingon, Elvish, or Esperanto, or those with piercings, tattoos, or unusually colored hair.

Olaniyi would never have gone to a Renfair on her own; she was supposed to be taking her at-risk group of kids from Baltimore by bus to the festival near Annapolis. As so often happened, after she spent most of the week booking the bus and obtaining the funds to go, then got herself up early on a Saturday, none of her kids showed. She already had a few tickets, and she was awake anyway, so she went on her own.

For the first hour, she stood to the side and gawked at the costumes. She also noted the lack of other dark skin. Many white women had braided their hair, which Olaniyi supposed she couldn't really call appropriation, since it was quasi-historical. The revelers walked around carrying wedges of cheesecake or giant turkey legs, which seemed to act as surrogates for the period weapons the signs at the front prohibited them from carrying. Many wore costumes that could only be considered "Renaissance" in the loosest of terms. Some were Shakespeare characters, some medieval wenches or knights. There were also pirates, and a few who might have been going for Robin Hood. She saw a dozen kilts. One reveler wore gold paint and a toga with grapes around his neck. Another was dressed as Batman.

She was thinking of bailing early on the thing when Jack and his wandering minstrels found her standing alone, swatting at bees behind a trash can overflowing with lemonade cups.

He wore a yellow, velvet suit sprouting a hundred buttons as he wandered the fairgrounds with a pipe and viol player (Connor and Steve, Olaniyi would later learn). They were an itinerant act, roving through the crowded alleys, stopping here and there when someone wanted to take a video of them. They mostly clowned around playing bawdy numbers, although they were in the middle of *Greensleeves* when Olaniyi first saw them.

It was a dull song, and the air was hot, because she'd come to opening weekend in August when the tickets were cheaper. Nobody seemed interested in the music; rather, they were annoyed that the wandering minstrels were blocking the alleys and slowing up traffic. The band decided to take a break and moved to the side, where Olaniyi ceased to notice them.

She watched a group sitting at a picnic table, five or six costumed younger people. They were all men except for one very tall, very overweight woman wearing a peasant's dress with the strings of her too-small bodice tied just enough so the nipples of her swollen breasts did not quite spill out. Olaniyi counted eleven earrings. The group looked like they were in the middle of their Christmas morning. They laughed at everything. Olaniyi wished Roberta were there with her to make fun of them.

When Jack and his minstrels struck up a song again, they were directly beside Olaniyi. They'd gotten close without her noticing, and now they were singing directly to her. Jack took the lead with the lyrics. He had close-cropped hair with a patch in the front he spiked with gel. His eyes were somewhat close together and gave him an aura of either eccentricity or wisdom, she couldn't tell. He sang a song about a man who convinces a young maiden to lie with him, called *"Watkin's Ale."* Olaniyi would hear all eight verses of it later, at Jack's house in the basement where he made lutes, but that day, they sang only the first two verses, ending on *"and gave her well of Watkin's Ale."* With that, Jack handed her a plastic cup filled with a flax-colored liquid and swept his hand downward with a bow. Olaniyi realized she was being recorded by more than one onlooker.

Since it seemed unlikely he would be drugging her in front of so many people, she drank it. It was sweet. He called it a bee sting, a mix of mead and cider. She'd have a hundred more of them in the next two months. That day, because the turkey leg she'd tried to eat hadn't tasted good and her stomach was empty, she felt lifted by the drink almost immediately. Before Jack and the minstrels were done with *"The Jovial Lass,"* Olaniyi was thinking of diving into the bosom of the woman at the table who sat laughing with her friends. That seemed to be the center of the spirit of the festival. She thought that if she were carried around in the woman's dress like a pendant and could watch the festival from there, suddenly all the jokes would seem funny to her, too.

Instead, she followed around after Jack and the minstrels at Jack's invitation, through the lanes and past all the pubs and stages. After an hour, she knew the layout cold. It had seemed overwhelmingly large when she first looked at the map at the gate, but soon she felt she could drop the map and go from memory. Jack and the minstrels—who had never developed a group name—finished their work for the day, leaving it to another itinerant band of musicians. Jack asked if Olaniyi wanted to join them as they wandered on their own. She practically dragged the three of them from one show to another, sometimes running from one to the next if the schedule was tight. When they passed a wine pavilion or a pub or a tavern, Jack got her another bee sting. She had to use the privies, which were just port-a-johns, seven times, but was too drunk to mind. It was a golden day. She was one girl among three boys, which made her unique. She was one of the only black faces at the festival, which made her more special still.

She watched swordsmiths and acrobats and two actors who staged a fake duel that was just an excuse to lob strained puns at one another. She cheered for the knights wearing the colors of the section she was sitting in at the joust. During the presentation of a glass blower who encouraged audience participation, she answered his question "Do you know what I'm tired of seeing?" by shouting out "white people," and gotten what seemed a good number of laughs. The glass blower gave her a bottle.

At the end of the day, she was too drunk to drive, so she went home with Jack. When she fell into bed with him, she figured he'd end up telling them all about it, so it was like making love to all of them at once.

She went back every weekend in September and into early October.

"Renaissance" was a catch-all term. It could be anything, as long as it was vaguely old, foreign, or weird. She could be anyone she wanted. She raced into the past and the future at once—studying Elizabethan history to win trivia games at the fair while also thinking already of marriage with Jack. She'd always worried that her boyfriends were either too American for her parents or not American enough. She could never tell whether their instinct to pass along their Yoruba heritage was stronger or their desire for her to be fully American and succeed. With Jack, she didn't have to decide what to be. They could just change costumes and be whatever they felt like being.

It was perfect until she introduced Jack to Roberta.

The three of them met at the same Guatemalan restaurant where Olaniyi and Roberta had been hanging out for years. Roberta refused to go anywhere else. She thought nearly all other restaurants were fake. With her, restaurants were either run by peasants with dirt from home still under their nails, or they were as phony as Outback. Olaniyi worried about bringing Jack into the place that had been their exclusive hangout. Roberta could be territorial. But Olaniyi also wanted to see how Jack fit into the rest of her life. She wanted Roberta to see that there could be room for him, and all the things that had existed between them as friends would still be there.

Roberta sat next to Olaniyi in the booth, so Jack had to sit alone across from them. She called the lute the flute, then the "skin flute." Jack laughed, but his laughter was perfunctory, like he'd heard that joke before. She said that Renfairs had nothing to do with the Renaissance and had no sense of historical accuracy. She said Jakob Burkhardt had invented the term Renaissance to mean a rebirth of antiquity, but it was a flawed term, because many of the things he thought were being reborn had, in fact, never left. Jack shrugged and said he figured the point was to have fun and maybe get people interested in something they hadn't been interested in before. There was plenty of time afterwards to learn the truth about things.

Roberta asked how Jack felt about dating a Nigerian girl and what he thought of her parents. She launched into thirty minutes on the history of the Yoruba Kingdom. It was all news to Olaniyi, who had never placated her parents by taking even one course on the history of any place within a thousand miles of where they had grown up.

History wasn't the only subject she'd been light on in college, which left her with a feeling she only vaguely understood the world. She'd majored in Women's Studies, where she met Roberta, who minored in it. They'd read Vagina Monologues together on Valentine's Day one year, and experimented with kissing each other and touching one another's breasts over the shirt another time. To Olaniyi, it felt like a prerequisite for graduating in her major to try at least once, and she was glad it had been with Roberta. They both laughed about it now, although Olaniyi didn't like to mention how she'd come as she straddled Roberta's knee, pressing against her blue stockings while they kissed. Olaniyi hadn't returned the favor, and had felt for years that she owed Roberta.

At dinner, Roberta brought up the night of kissing and petting, with a lot more details than Olaniyi had told Jack to prepare him. She added details Olaniyi wasn't sure had really happened, and as she talked, she pressed her body next to Olaniyi. Roberta was solid, dense. Olaniyi had run track in high school, and still did reasonably well in the 5K races she ran a few times a year, but Roberta had thrown the javelin.

To Jack's credit, Olaniyi didn't think he was aroused by Roberta flirting with her. Most guys would have already been angling for a threesome. Roberta was pretty, in her muscular way. She wore the best hair of anyone Olaniyi knew. Jack just sat in his seat, sipping unsweetened iced tea, because he was driving them all home. Maybe he sensed it was a trap.

He nearly made it through the night without earning any more disdain from Roberta than he'd had coming in, but then Roberta asked if he liked raspberries and Jack sat there, looking dumb for thirty seconds.

"So, do you like raspberries?" she asked again.

"I don't know how to answer that," he said.

"What do you mean, you don't know how to answer it?"

"Well, I guess I'm middle of the road. So middle of the road, in fact, I don't even know how to answer the question."

"Then why didn't you just say that?" she asked, and took the check from the middle of the table, although Jack had already placed his credit card on top of it.

For weeks after, Roberta would not let up on the subject of Jack. She called Olaniyi a groupie for a flute player. She questioned Olaniyi when she swore the sex was good when she couldn't see how it could be. Mostly, she refused to let Jack's silence on the raspberry question die. Why had he stood there like he was meditating when she'd asked him a simple question?

Olaniyi had to admit, it had been a strange blip in Jack's otherwise steady-seeming character. She put the question to him. Jack said he'd suspected Roberta wanted to get him some kind of drink with raspberries in it. The question had come out of thin air, so he'd assumed she had a reason for asking it. He didn't want her to buy him a shot. He didn't want her to buy him anything. He didn't want to feel like he owed her.

The last weekend of Renfair, in mid-October, Olaniyi finally managed to get three of her kids to wake up on a Saturday to come with her. Ranae was dating Jaquawn, and they came together. DeShawn came alone. Olaniyi had been with the non-profit in Baltimore for three years, first as a poorly paid, post-college associate just glad to have some sort of job with her Women's Studies degree, now as a slightly less poorly paid director of activities.

Ranae was pregnant. It might have been Jaquawn's; Olaniyi was hazy on that. DeShawn wore the same sweatshirt he'd worn every time she'd ever seen him. It said, "No Bad Days." Jack was fun and easy with the kids. He let them try to play his lute. His band played a version of Beyonce's "All the Single Ladies" for them. The kids didn't like it, because it was an old song, but they pretended to. The drunk group in Viking costumes loved it. DeShawn wanted to come learn to make lutes, and he meant it. He was happy to do anything that got him out of his house.

That left Sunday, the last day of the fair, the day Olaniyi had invited her parents to come.

"It'll all end soon after Sunday, you'll see," Roberta told her. "I'm glad you had a fun little fantasy, but it will end after the fair is over. He's not the right guy for you."

Olaniyi made a mistake. When her parents asked what the Renaissance Fair was, she said it was a place where people wore clothes from a long time ago in order to celebrate the past. When Jack and Olaniyi pulled up to the curb to pick them up, her mom was wearing a giant purple *gele* on her head. Her father had on a yellow and red striped *agbada* over his clothes. It was like cultural day at middle school all over again, the day Olaniyi had tried to keep hidden from her parents but they'd found out about anyway.

"Mom, this isn't a festival for African things!" she cried.

"Nonsense, girl," her mother told her. "You said people wear old things and celebrate old culture. Our culture is older than anything from Europe."

44

"It's fine," Jack said. "They'll fit right in."

"I'm pretty sure that whatever the opposite of fitting in is, that's what they'll do."

Just trust me. Roberta had said. *I know you. This isn't real. It's a mistake.*

Jack was right. They fit right in. Her mother's *gele* was purple. People thought she was a wizard. Or a jester. Or they knew it was Nigerian, and they thought it was even better because of that. Her father tried a bee sting. He'd never had any alcohol ever, as far as Olaniyi knew. When Jack and his band started to play *"Watkin's Ale,"* her mom and dad started to dance the traditional dance Olaniyi thought was called the *Bata*. It seemed ridiculous to Olaniyi without the drums that usually accompanied it, but again, the revelers disagreed. They cheered her parents. It was the largest crowd she'd ever seen gather around Jack's band. It was impossible to get by. Jack smiled at her as his band laughed through the lyrics.

At the privies, a text from Roberta: *You don't owe me anything. You can do what you want. I'm telling you this as your friend.*

Roberta came from a home as bad as any that Olaniyi's kids lived in. She put herself through school, became a nurse, and bought a house by age twenty-four. She had been the one to give Olaniyi money when her car died right after college. Olaniyi's parents didn't have the money to help; her father drove a cab, and they'd spent everything they'd ever saved to send her to college. Roberta had never asked to be paid back, never so much as brought it up. She said helping people out was part of the real world, and so was taking help when you needed it.

Olaniyi's father paid attention to everything Jack had to say about the lute and about late medieval music. Given an audience that took him seriously, Jack seemed somehow more authoritative, more in charge. His jaw seemed more set. He'd just gotten a haircut, and he seemed so masculine, he could have been holding a rugby ball as much as a stringed instrument.

Another text. *We've known each other a long time now, O. If I didn't love you so much, I'd tell you what you want to hear. Because I care about you, I'm telling you the truth.*

It was the first real week of color in the leaves. If possible, it was even more enchanted than the first week she'd been there. Whatever fairy tale they'd been living in, it wouldn't let up until the very last moment of the very last day of the fair. She wasn't even drunk, because she didn't feel like drinking around her parents, but that just made it feel, if anything, more other-worldly to travel the grounds sober.

Whatever was not clear about the future, it seemed pretty sure that her parents would not be an obstacle to her and Jack. Her father draped his arm around him and Connor and called them both "okay." Everything about the relationship had gone well so far, other than Roberta's warnings. Roberta usually warned Olaniyi about everything, although Roberta claimed that was because most things really weren't all they seemed. It was important to kick the tires on things and see if they really were what they said they were. What would happen when the festival season ended and the time to kick the tires came for Jack and Olaniyi?

Her dad wanted to head to the axe throwing range, and Jack and the band obliged him. It was a popular spot. The guys who ran the axe gallery were better looking than your average carnie—they were among the kilt-wearing crowd and weren't unpleasant to look at while wearing them—and they did offer a few decent prizes. There was a suit of chain mail Jack said he liked that you could get for hitting the bullseye with all five axes. But throwing axes, Olaniyi had found, was harder than shooting ducks or throwing rings on bottles. She'd spent fifteen dollars one Saturday and thrown until her arm gave out, but hadn't even managed to get a single axe to stick in the target.

Her father was hurling axes erratically at the target. Most were missing wildly. One stuck in the wrong target. The men in kilts running the show laughed nervously; Olaniyi wasn't sure if they were amused or afraid he would hurt someone. A sign said that nobody who appeared intoxicated was allowed to play, but even Olaniyi couldn't tell if her dad was drunk or just excited. He didn't get out much.

Jack nudged Olaniyi, his arms folded across himself.

"We should get some axes and a target and practice in the back yard for the next year," he said. "We can come back here and rob them blind."

Next year. If she came back next year with Jack, it would be different. Nothing would be new. Things she'd found funny this year would be annoying the next. She wouldn't come every weekend, that's for sure. They'd spend weekends apart while he played with his friends. She'd reconnect with Roberta, who'd say she guessed she'd been wrong, and was glad it worked out, after all.

Olaniyi's mother took a turn and missed everything. None of her throws made it halfway to the target. One of the kilted men gave her a plush dragon. Her mom cheered and raised it over her head.

"Better than holding onto everything all winter," Olaniyi heard the man tell another attendant.

Her parents had always been happy to take what had been given them, but had taught Olaniyi to hope for more, to keep hacking away until she hit quintuple bull's eyes and came away with the chain mail. Roberta, meanwhile, would say the chain mail was a lie meant to take money from suckers. If you wanted chain mail, you had to go out and work hard to buy your own, not expect it to come to you from luck.

Jack had come to her by luck. Was he a lie?

She wanted to leave the axe range, but also wanted to never leave the festival. She didn't want to answer whether Alphas and Betas was an important distinction in men, and if so, what Jack was. She didn't want to figure out if Jack was a mistake. She didn't want to have to decide between what was right and what was fun, between being gay or being straight, between what was real and what was fake. Between owing someone for something and having her freedom.

She liked that Roberta called her "O." A name is just one name, but an initial can be lots of things. A circle can start and end anywhere.

She paid the man who'd given her mother the stuffed dragon, took her five axes. She handed them to Jack.

"One round, last of the year," she said.

He stepped up to the line, jiggled the handle a bit to get the weight of it.

She whispered in his ear, "If you don't get at least one to stick in the target, we're through after today." She kissed his ear. "No pressure."

He brought the axe up straight over his head, trying to keep his arm from bending, like he'd seen on YouTube. He wanted to keep his wrist from flexing, but he couldn't stop his own instinct. He threw the first one right of the mark.

"You can do it!" Olaniyi's mother yelled to him.

He threw a second. This time he aimed left of where he had the first time. Olaniyi saw him shift his body. He got the horizontal portion right, but his toss came up short. It whacked into the wood beneath the target and spun to the ground.

It seemed as good a way for Olaniyi to make a decision as any other. Her parents had been an arranged marriage. The third shot went over the target. Her father cheered him on.

He might get one in. They'd played before, and he'd managed to get a few to stick. Not that often for all the axes he'd thrown, but a few hits. Something in his body changed on the fourth throw. He seemed more comfortable, or maybe more determined. The axe head hit the target and bounced off, tumbling backwards to the ground. Her parents groaned.

"You had it!"

Olaniyi turned from Jack as he readied for his final throw. She would know without needing to look what had happened. She would know what the future held when she heard the sound. She would listen for either another disappointed groan from her parents, or the deep note of metal hitting something solid and sticking.

- Jacob Weber

Some Far Star

What I am drinking now is poison.
–General Slobodan Praljak, after denying he was
guilty of war crimes, The Hauge, 11/29/17

When he pleaded for a small bottle
of stellar light from some far star, I knew
what it could do. How it thrashes the brain.
Throttles and breaches the heart. How it can't

be stilled or killed. But, tell me, who was I
to deny him his final performance?
Wanton light undulating his tongue. His
accusatory eyes, too wet, too bright.

I know. You condemn me. You demand I
crawl inside that open vial, listen
to my heart dissolve, again and again.
But, my friend, didn't I deliver him

a dram of justice? I let the old fool
die like an old fool. Just as we wanted.

- John Bradley

The Color of War

That shrapnel scar tissue, those ribbed furrows, I asked him if I could
place my finger there and there.

Visible, in that summer moment, at dinner.

We sleep in language, no one said, not fully awake or asleep.

The beer foam in his German beer glass dissolving,
as foam will do.

Surprised that he allowed me, my flesh, to press against his
flesh.

I can almost remember him telling me how he had only summer clothes
that winter in the Ardennes. How he dressed in a sheet to resemble snow.

My finger, for two full seconds, on his war. The future of fuscia.

War is the most noble sport, I might have said then, horrible to say.

But no author can be completely responsible, you might have replied,
for what drops
into his lingual field.

Fail to mention: His hands smelling of Babo, Ajax, Dutch Boy.

Fail to mention: The future smoldering, in an ashtray, of my Vietnam-war-era
draft card.

Fail to mention: The reader of this artifact as another artifact. Saith the man
vacuuming his feet, eyes, mouth.

Thus: The colon disappearing into the ant, the ant thus
disappearing.

Into: The color of war.

- John Bradley

Behind a Locked Door: Brief Interview with Covid-19

Q. Will there be dancing and embracing in the near future?
A. When your face is a collage, everyone recognizes you.

Q. When will it be safe to breathe near another who is also breathing?
A. If it rains, let the rain rain, infected by beauty.

Q. Do you enjoy your work?
A. Simplicity is a circle ending in an inky knot.

Q. There will be laughter and forgetfulness in the near future?
A. A monk once asked his teacher What is the Buddha? The teacher replied:
Buddha is the shit stick.

Q. When will I be able to hold my body against the body of a friend?
A. I can only teach you what I don't know.

Q. If I think about you, I try not to. If I try not to, I think about you.
A. Inside a potato, a flight of stairs leading to a door. It is locked. There, the moon waits for you.

Q. What message are you trying to tell us?
A. You know that orange peel in the shape of an ear can hear everything you say.

Q. Do you enjoy your work?
A. I want nothing more than to sit and gaze at the apple blossoms.

Q. If I think about you, I try not to. If I try not to, I think about you.
A. Alfred Hitchcock, they say, was afraid of the dark.

Q. Must I one day forgive you?
A. In the house of silence, every sound is a bell.

- John Bradley

Dear Bog Man

For Tollund Man, 4th Century BCE, Denmark
after a photograph by Arne Mikkelsen

Let me, if I might, loosen that leather rope pulled so tight
around your throat. Soothe those steep furrows in your brow.

For a moment stroke your bronzed, too-taut flesh, stretched
across brittle bone. Through centuries of boggy sleep

you've travelled. Eyes and mouth closed. Head wrapped
in leather cap. Hair, leather, flesh—all dyed red by bitter bog

water. Tell us: When that rope—woven for you, only for you—
cinched ever tighter. Tight around your throat. What goddess,

what tree-born creature did you beseech? What fevered words
burbled past your lips? Tell us, who bore you to the brooding

bog? Whose hand pulled shut your eyes, your mouth? Cast
you into fetal repose? Eased you down into the wakeful water?

Dear Bog Man, how deep you've sunken into my sleep. Still
at night, I can hear your shrunken heart beat:

Slip this rope around your empty throat. Don't fear. The bog
is but a portal. Ever so gently, I shall draw you through.

- John Bradley

The Weather on Mars

Whenever I hear someone say *particulate,* I feel fireflies
stirring in my belly. Sleep ends where oblivion's tongue
rends and upends and begins. It got to the point where
Thoreau could pick up a pebble and read the weather
on Mars. Back when we spoke in bird and bramble
and berry. *An injured comet is still a comet,* says the eye
surgeon. The skeleton carried a guitar case with a polished
femur inside. Pieces of Iceland can be found most days
in a discarded plastic bottle. The music at the top
of the tree swells up to the roots of the tree. False
or obscenely true: *My white-haired father used to be
mistaken long ago for The Man from Glad.* Sally
the immortal feral cat heard a bird call that smelled
of moon, ice, tar; she skedaddled. Tender the bottom
of your feet; weather if you can the brain. Lenny Bruce
once performed as Bruce Lenny; no one could tell
the difference. The fox made of wood shavings and
barbed wire doesn't chase rabbits; it hunts the green
angel that lives in the chimney. Where the world begins
and rends and upends. She told me she wanted to be
a crone; I aspire to be a troglodyte, I told her. In art
school, I studied forgery; I could make Pablo Picasso's
signature look phony. Pieces of Iceland can be seen
any discarded day on YouTube. *We are meteors
that leave no trace,* says Lorca's missing rib.
Or did it say, *I can't find my own carcass.* A piece
of broccoli stuck to the cold sidewalk. *I only want to
whirl,* said the whorl. Tell me what you told me
on Mars. Back when we spoke in bird and bramble
and berry. Come back, Federico, heal us, hurt
us. *Throat star magma,* repeats Radio Thoreau.

- John Bradley

Bone Weight

My **late father used to make a living as a fortune teller.** He called himself a calculator of fates and read fortunes by weighing bones. This was not a weight in kilogrammes or pounds, but an astrological weight based on the circumstances of one's birth. According to my father's Tong Shu almanac, heavy bones foretold a good life. They were dense with marrow and rich in celestial calcium, strong enough to weather hard knocks and march through life unmolested. Light-boned people, on the other hand, hovered on the edges of existence, insubstantial and easily broken.

As a child, I had wondered if the predictions in my father's almanac applied only to Chinese people the way some heavens were open only to followers of certain gods. My father had chastised me for my ignorance. Bone weight did not depend on skin colour or preferred choice of heaven. What mattered were the variables of birth that determined the quality of one's earthly life: year, month, day, hour, and gender.

Meeting Lakshmi reminded me of my father's faith in his almanac. She lived in a block of low-cost flats, the type where people threw their babies' used diapers out their windows and the stairwells stank of urine. People like Lakshmi and her husband Thagaraj must have bones the weight of rice husks. Their marrow must be as dry and friable as the leaves that Thagaraj swept off the roads when he was alive.

I rattled the padlock on her metal grille door and called out, "Hello, Lakshmi!"

She appeared from behind a curtain and said, "Are you here to help me, miss? Or have you come to harass me?"

I was surprised by the lack of niceties. I was not a two-bit goon sent to threaten her, but I let it pass. My job was to broker a win-win solution. Surely that counted as help, not harassment. I flashed a winning smile and said, "To help you, of course." Although she did not smile back, she unlocked her door. I stepped through the doorway into her flat. Half a flat, actually. A tarpaulin sheet with a picture of a celebrity advertising a skin whitening cream divided what was one home into two. Lakshmi's half had no windows and reeked of cumin, onions, and cooking oil. She gestured for me to sit on one of the chairs near the door. Her chairs—cheap, plastic, with legs prone to buckling—were familiar. They were identical to the ones in my father's old house. I sat carefully and breathed lightly.

She offered me a cup of water which I had to take from her hands because there was no table between us. I thanked her and put it on the floor. I wiped my fingers on my skirt while she watched me with wary, red-veined eyes. Her hair was an uncombed tangle, white from her roots to her ears and black from her ears to her shoulders. It was as if she had black hair one day and started growing white the next.

She said, "Have you seen the video, miss?"

I said, "I have seen a bit of it, yes." I had watched the video fifteen times, all nine minutes of it. I stopped flinching after the third time.

"I saw everything. I remember everything." She twisted and untwisted the hem of her blouse with a twig of a finger. I was glad that the door was open. I would make a quick exit if she became hysterical.

The day of the video was the first day of Chinese New Year. Thagaraj's employer had given him a leaf blower, a contraption with a bazooka muzzle and a two-stroke gasoline engine to be shouldered like a backpack. Thagaraj had boarded his work van with eleven other workers and the men were distributed to various streets in affluent neighbourhoods. They were put to work that public holiday morning because it was customary for Chinese families who lived in houses to give angpows to postmen, garbage collectors, road sweepers, and security guards during Chinese New Year. I did the same every year. A token generosity of ten or twenty ringgit in a few angpows cleared my conscience and saved me from worrying about lost mail or uncollected garbage.

Had it been any other holiday, one without the lure of money, Thagaraj would have enjoyed an ordinary day at home with Lakshmi. Instead, fate swept him up, deposited him on Lorong Merah at nine o'clock one bright morning, and left him there with an appetite for angpows.

Lorong Merah was a sedate and pretty street lined with trees. The house owners had planted frangipani, tecoma, bucida, mango, jackfruit, papaya, avocado, and palm trees outside their fences. When frangipani and tecoma bloomed, more extravagantly during the lunar new year than at other times, a touch of spring and celebration coloured the street in pinks, whites, and purples. Those trees had given Thagaraj a regular job. They shed an abundance of leaves and confetti petals every day to be swept up and bagged.

Thagaraj might have been excited by the leaf blower in his hands. Brandishing a machine instead of a broom would have felt like an upgrade. The leaf blower had a motor that emitted a throaty 90-decibel growl. When revved, it roared at 120 decibels which was louder than a passing Harley-Davidson. It was loud enough to tell the residents of Lorong Merah that he was outside their homes and ready to receive their largesse on that auspicious day.

If he had used his old coconut lidi broom, he would not have triggered the events of the day. The rasp of a broom, a gentle and reassuring sound, would have soaked into the mundane, suburban babble of morning birdcalls and wakening households. Instead, he lingered longer than he should have outside a house with two red lanterns hanging in the car porch. He had not known that angpows were not forthcoming from this household that put up decorations as a show of solidarity during festivals: a pair of lanterns during Chinese New Year, a Christmas tree, a few paper garlands and cardboard cut-outs of oil lamps during Deepavali, and a veritable light show during Hari Raya.

The man of the house with the lanterns, Tuan Za, had been in a video call with an overseas client when his negotiations were sullied by Thagaraj's thundering leaf blower. Tuan Za had come out of his house wearing a tie and jacket over his chequered sarong and slippers. He had yelled at Thagaraj, probably calling him many names. 'Senile old man' had surely been one of them. Thagaraj was fifty-five years old and looked a decade older. Perhaps keling had been another; Tuan Za used this insult frequently in our office. Or pariah. Or other common Tamil vulgarities.

If Thagaraj had bowed his head and switched off his leaf blower, perhaps he would still be alive. Knowing when to bow was important. A well-timed bow could soothe heated tempers and bruised egos. But he had not bowed. Maybe the machine had emboldened him. Maybe he had gunned the engine to drown out the profanities spewing from Tuan Za's mouth. I imagined that in a brief, reckless moment of agency, Thagaraj had let his leaf blower speak for him in a wordless, 120-decibel fuck-you exhalation of air. It was an impulse I could understand, one I had learnt to swallow. Swallowing put money in the pocket; earned a good word in a well-placed ear; secured bonuses, promotions, trips abroad, cars, houses, and jobs for friends and relatives.

Still, road sweepers did not go around looking to start arguments. Thagaraj retreated to the next house, the one with the CCTV cameras that had recorded the damning video. His turned back would have been an affront to Tuan Za who expected docile submission from someone like Thagaraj, a common road sweeper of little consequence. Tuan Za conceded only to men more powerful than him. I knew that for a fact. He tolerated those who yielded and punished those who resisted. Underlings mollified him with praise and said: *Yes, Tuan. Right away, Tuan. No problem, Tuan. Jump? How high, Tuan?* But Thagaraj was unschooled in the responses that could have bought him mercy.

Of course, what had happened off-camera was conjecture. *This* was in the video: Tuan Za runs after Thagaraj. He looks surprisingly nimble in his sarong and slippers. He seizes the leaf blower and hits Thagaraj with the long end of the machine. Once, twice. Three, four, five times in an escalating rage. Thagaraj flails his arms against the blows. He falls to the ground, entangled in his machinery. Tuan Za grabs a neighbour's garbage bin, a big one with wheels. He slams Thagaraj seven times with the wheeled end. The remains of a reunion dinner from the night before scatter like scraps flung at strays. Thagaraj stops moving. A wheel rolls away in a comic detail. Tuan Za unknots his sarong and fastens it again like a man who has just finished a meal. He checks his jacket for stains and brushes something off a sleeve. Then, he turns and walks away. Thagaraj lies at a crooked angle; his back arches over the motor

56

on his back. Blood from his cracked skull leaks onto the driveway tiles. In the black and white CCTV footage, his white hair blackens. His blood is as dark as his skin.

This was the 'everything' that Lakshmi said she remembered, the last nine minutes of her husband's life.

From where Lakshmi and I were sitting, I could see a framed photograph of Thagaraj on the only table in their flat, wreathed in decaying jasmines. He was much younger in the photograph than the man in the video; his hair was black and his face sombre. His bone weight must have been that of the paper his last photograph was printed on. A few grammes. Not even an ounce. His was the throwaway weight of a life that could be extinguished by a garbage bin in the time it would take to boil an egg.

My father came to mind again. As I grew older, every encounter with mortality revived memories of him. My father was a poor fortune teller who had lived off the petty problems of other people's lives. For a fee, he had delivered prayers and offerings to temple deities for customers who were too busy to pray. He had been a proxy worshipper. A runner for the gods. I was like my father now—an envoy. I offered enticement to Lakshmi in exchange for a withdrawal of the police report made against Tuan Za. A carton of Mandarin oranges and a tin of love letters that I had brought as gifts were on an upturned bucket. But Lakshmi was no goddess. She was only a malnourished, brittle woman worn thin by life and mourning.

I said, "Tuan Za sent me. He wants to help you and he has suggested thirty thousand ringgit."

"I want him to apologise. Money," she said, "is not important."

Money was all-important, *thangachi.* I said, "I apologise on his behalf. I'm his representative."

"Ask him to come here himself. Tell him to look in my eyes and say he was wrong. Face to face. Tell him to stand there in front of Thagaraj's picture and ask for forgiveness."

Tuan Za was not going to step out of his chauffeur-driven BMW, walk up four flights of rubbish-strewn stairs, and apologise to the widow of a road sweeper. He was not even going to touch a telephone with Lakshmi on the other end.

"Lakshmi, Tuan Za is not coming here. You have to be realistic. Like I said, I apologise for Tuan."

"Miss, you didn't kill my husband. What for you say sorry unless you tell me you carry his sins for him?" Who did she think she was, this woman who looked like charred wood? What big statements were these coming from her gap-toothed mouth?

"You're asking for words. Words are nothing. He can pay people to close this case and you'll get nothing. Zero. *Kosong.* You might as well take

57

the thirty thousand before he changes his mind."

"My husband was doing his job. It's wrong that he was killed just for doing his job. It's not fair. He was just doing his job."

My father used to say that the secret of the universe was balance. Birds lived in the sky, fish in the sea. Light and dark. Yin and yang. That is why some simpletons were blessed with joy, and people who were too intelligent or beautiful had punishing lives. Look at Stephen Hawking, he offered. Or Marilyn Monroe. My father had been as naïve as Lakshmi with her cries of unfairness. Those were meaningless examples, convenient placebos to cure us of envy.

The balance of my father's universe, as he saw it, was a set of self-correcting scales see-sawing over countless lives and infinite lifetimes until it reached equilibrium. My father was mistaken. The idea of retribution or correction of wrongs in a next life was just a falsity to take the sting out of injustices. The real way of the universe was imbalance. It was not a set of scales, but a pendulum. An amusement park ride gone wild that swung in ever increasing arcs. Entropy prevailed over all else and we swung faster and faster from one disaster to the next. Light-boned people were thrown off earlier, that was all. If there was any balance at all, it was that of victim versus victimizer, prey versus predator, weak versus strong. There was not the slightest aspect of a Monroe or Hawking in the lives of people like Lakshmi and Thagaraj, not by any stretch of the imagination.

Here was the duplicity of my father's profession. He had prescribed remedies: an incantation written on yellow paper, folded into a small triangle, and carried in the wallet for protection against harm; an offering of a whole, steamed chicken and a slab of roast pork; a dragon and phoenix jade pendant to be worn for marital harmony. If someone could not afford jade, he offered resin replicas. He had something at the right price for everyone. If his customer's circumstances improved, say a divorce averted or a job secured, my father claimed to be the agent of success. To disgruntled customers, he said, "It is fated. Nobody can influence a predetermined future."

That was the handy escape clause of his profession. Every outcome was fait accompli. He had believed in the certainty of fate while peddling cures to cheat it, but my father was not a conman. Neither was he malicious. A person was not always wrong when belief and action were not congruent. Everything was context, and context was malleable. I had to tell Lakshmi that there was no black and white resolution for her. The best outcome was a mutually agreed grey. Thirty-thousand-ringgit worth of grey.

I said, "Do you believe in fate, Lakshmi?"

"Miss, yes. I believe but ..."

I put up my hand. "Good. It's good that we believe in the same thing. What is done is done. If you accept this money, you'll have closure. You don't need to drag this out or worry about it anymore. Just accept that this is fate."

"Miss, don't talk like that. I'm a simple woman, not as clever as you, but maybe I'm not stupid. It's fate for my husband to die, but fate is not telling me to shut my mouth. And please don't tell me that murderers will be punished in another life. If we believe that, everyone will rob and murder today. If I believe that, I can put a knife in my husband's killer tomorrow. I know where he lives. I can put a knife in your eye now."

There was a new light in her eyes, and I worried that the situation was not as simple as I had expected. Maybe some meddling do-gooder had gotten to her and planted lofty notions of justice in her head.

"Calm down, Lakshmi. Let me tell you about Tuan Za. He's not an evil man. Yes, he's impatient because he's very busy. He lost his temper with your husband. That's all, and he is sorry. He told me that himself. He didn't have bad intentions. He has many companies and if he goes to jail, five hundred workers will lose their jobs. Some of them are from Indonesia, Nepal, Bangladesh. From India. Poor people. Some of them are the only ones working to feed their families back home."

"Miss, you say he is not a bad man. Is he a good man? My husband was a good man. Is this Tuan of yours a better man because he has many workers and pays your salary?"

Being poor did not automatically make Thagaraj a better man. A widow's judgement did not make a man a saint. In fact, I had no idea what kind of a man he was. I said, "Children, Lakshmi. Tuan Za has three children; one is just a baby. Three children will lose their father. You will cause their suffering, Lakshmi, because you are too proud to take the money that is good for you. Is this what Thagaraj would have wanted? To cause more misery to other families?"

"Does your Tuan's wife deserve more happiness than me because she has children? More peace? Does she ask herself why she is happy the same way I ask myself why my life is harder than a stone? Tell me, miss."

My cell phone beeped. There was a message from Tuan Za's office. It read: *50K max. Don't waste time. Boss said got bigger fish to fry.*

I said, "Who are we to judge whether people deserve what they have? Let's make it forty thousand, Lakshmi. You can do a lot of good with forty thousand. Think about who you can help." I thought about what I could do with ten thousand ringgit.

She said, "I am poor, I know. I am uneducated. But don't play me, miss."

"I was also poor. I know what it's like. When I was young, my father did not have much money, but I managed to finish university. Look at me now. I'm doing well. I can take care of my family. Accept the money, Lakshmi. You can send two boys to university in Thagaraj's name. They can make a living for their families. They will kiss your feet and sing your praises for the rest of their lives."

I was not lying. We had been poor when I was growing up. Not as poor as Lakshmi but poor for a Chinese family. Poor enough for me to be embarrassed that we lived in a brick and plank new village house, that our Honda was a Cub and not a Civic, that there were no weekly trips to the movies and malls, or holidays abroad in cold countries. Fortune telling had brought my father no fortune.

This was how I imagined my father's work: There is a room which holds all of a person's life. There is a window that fogs up constantly. The person outside the room has to keep wiping the window if he wants to see through it. The contents of the room remain the same but the effort of keeping the window clear drains the seer's energy.

Fortune telling was like that, like cleaning other people's windows with one's chi. Divining the fates of others had eroded my father's life. It was the inverse observer effect at work. Since the object being observed—the predetermined future—was immutable, the act of observing altered the observer instead. When my father died, my mother said he was so depleted that the breeze from the ceiling fan had wafted him off the bed. This was an exaggeration, of course, but not far from the truth. His dying had been a slow fading away as if the sums of his own life were a continuous series of subtractions.

I was no calculator of fates. I would watch safely from the side lines while Tuan Za tugged the puppet strings around him and clouded the window into Thagaraj's life and death. He had sent me here as a parallel thread in his plans. I would earn some favour if I resolved the matter with Lakshmi, but if I did not, he had alternative plans already set in motion. His people were talking to the police and the hospital. His machinery was working. One person connected to the next. Favours were being called in and pledged. A friendly coroner would testify to a less incriminating cause of death. Perhaps a cardiac arrest from the unaccustomed weight of the leaf blower. Drugs in the blood. An aneurysm. Thagaraj's employer could be coaxed to corroborate with a promise of new contracts. Maybe Thagaraj would develop a history of violent behaviour at work. Or an alcohol addiction and gang connections. Facts could be shaped. Good men could be created or unmade. It was a simple matter of who had the bigger balls, who owned the connections, and who had the heavier bones. The bones high up the hierarchy were ballasted with money and political clout until they were heavier than the law. Murder could be reduced to misadventure, and misadventure was as good as bad luck where no party was at fault. Lakshmi had sorry weapons in this fight; her arrows were made of straw. Her battle horse was a dead one.

I said, "Take the money, Lakshmi. This is a once in a lifetime opportunity. Thagaraj is not coming back, no matter what you do. Think of it this way. Maybe he died so that you can live better."

She was motionless. Her hands were on her lap. She seemed to have stopped breathing altogether. For a minute, she was a statue hewn from lava rock; her black and white hair a mark of divinity; her charcoal body forged by old fires. My oranges and cookies lay at her feet like meagre appeasement against unknown dangers.

She said, "If people go to university and grow up like you, better that they drop out of school and become road sweepers like my husband."

Touché, *thangachi*. I forced a laugh and said, "I will ask you again tomorrow. Think about it. Forty thousand ringgit, Lakshmi. Think about all the good you can do."

As I stood to leave, I knocked over the cup of water. It spread a dark puddle on the cement floor like Thagaraj's blood in the video. I bent to right the cup that had rolled to Lakshmi's feet, but I stopped myself. Flustered, I told myself that she was only an unfortunate woman who had run out of money for hair dye.

On the way out, I reminded myself that she was to be pitied, but instead of the swell of superiority that followed pity, I felt that my bones had been hollowed out. My knees were plastic joints threatening to fold under me. I gripped the banister as I hurried down the stairs littered with the debris of lives lived, nervous that Lakshmi might expel a breath and blow me tumbling down.

- **Shih-Li Kow**

Delinquent

The large black dildo sways back and forth. The elderly lady clutches her handbag and flees into the department store. Drew laughs and slaps the dildo against a bench.

Whack!

Passers-by stare our direction and then quickly look away once they realize the object being waved around is a large black dildo.

I light a cigarette because I don't know what else to do. I feel guilty about the elderly lady, which makes me restless.

"I'm fucken hungry" says Jared. "Subway?"

So, we walk into Subway. I don't order anything because I'm broke, and even if I wasn't, the variety of options intimidates me, and I wouldn't know what to order. My life skills are such that I don't even know how to construct a decent sandwich.

Our small group sits in a booth, while the manager glares at us from behind the counter.

"I heard you fingered Julia on the weekend" Jared says to Drew.

I feel uncomfortable. I live with my mum and sister and hearing women spoken about in such ways is foreign to me.

Jared gives Drew a high-five and then stares at me. My lack of response creates tension.

"Well, it's probably safer than the black dildo" I stammer.

The group laughs, which somehow makes them more animalistic. They start spraying soft drinks through straws. Various colours hit the windows and slide down like an abstract painting gone rogue.

"Do something" Drew demands, noticing I'm not partaking in the spontaneous vandalism of windows.

I reach into my pocket, light another cigarette and take a drag. Smoke fills the air of the restaurant and mixes with the sugary aroma coating the windows.

"That's it!" a middle-aged employee says. "You will have to leave. Smoking is not permitted in this venue."

"Okay then" I calmly respond, feeling a sense of relief at finally escaping the chaos. "I'm leaving."

"The rest of you need to leave too" she demands, staring at the windows.

I walk down the street and the rest of the group soon catches up.

"So, when are you next playing a gig?" Drew asks, tapping the dildo against his hand.

"Next Friday" I tell him.

"Cool" he says. "Have you heard of the band Anal Cunt?"

"Can't say I have" I laugh. "That's an interesting band name."

"They have this song called *Van Full of Retards*. You should check it out" he says.

I hear a sliding door swing open from a parked vehicle behind us.

"What the fuck did you say?" yells an angry-looking guy covered in tattoos. He stands beside a white van with tinted windows, accompanied by two other angry-looking guys also covered in tattoos. They appear as if they have just finished a vigorous session at the gym - complete with steroids.

"What the fuck did you say about my van you little pricks?" he yells.

"Run" I tell myself, as survival instincts kick in.

Our group separates as we escape in various directions. Drew panics and throws his dildo in a bush outside the local Baptist church. If I had time to pause and acknowledge their daily signage, I would discover it reads *It is far better to live out what the bible says rather than just quote it.* But I don't. I'm running for my life, and I don't know what the hell I'm living out these days anyway.

I stumble through a carpark, down an alleyway and across a field until I'm at the river's edge. Alone and breathing heavily. I gaze out to the river. I contemplate whether I could swim to the fishing boat bobbing up and down in the distance should the van people find me. I think back to primary school swim classes and how the teacher kept me in the shallow end with some kick-boards and an equally uncoordinated kid called Raphael.

"Not a fucking chance" I mutter.

***

The taste of lukewarm goon fills my mouth and makes me grimace. But I gulp down the cheap wine anyway, because I arrived here far too sober.

A loud knock on the door interrupts the quiet gathering taking place. The gathering is slowly turning into a party, so I walk to the door with Jess, whose house it is, to ensure there aren't any gate crashers.

It's Drew.

"Hi" he says, standing upright with a smile and appearing proud with himself.

"Hi" I slowly reply, as I try to process what I'm seeing. "Why do you have a dead possum on top of a tiki torch?"

"Well, I was walking past this restaurant and they looked pretty" he explains, with bloodshot eyes that admire his newfound accessory.

"I hope that poor thing was already dead" I say, gesturing to the life-less animal plonked atop his tiki torch.

"Yeah, I found old mate beside the road on the way here" he sighs.

"You can't bring that fucking thing inside!" orders Jess.

More people start to arrive at the party. They see the dead possum tiki torch and hesitate to walk any further.

"Um, we heard there was a party here?" one of them nervously says. Drew leers at them with his possum torch.

"Stop it, Drew!" Jess yells.

"Bloody hell, mate" I say. "We need to put that poor thing to rest." I grab the contraption from his hands. "Let go!"

"But it's my torch!" he argues.

Drew suddenly releases his grip and I lose my balance. I stumble sideways across the outdoor patio as I hopelessly wrestle control of the possum torch. I crash into the metal railing with a thud. The tiki torch abruptly wedges itself between the decking and railing. The momentum transforms the torch into a medieval catapult and sends the dead possum flying through the air and over the fence. It lands heavily on the next-door neighbour's roof below. *Whump!* Ceramic orange tiles dislodge from the roof. We watch in silence as they cascade one-by-one off the sloped roof and smash into pieces on the ground below.

"Shit" I gasp.

"What the hell?" Jess screams. "Get the fuck out of here – the lot of you!"

I find myself walking home. The dimly lit streets are deserted and quiet, except for Jared occasionally yelling "Do you like my new hat?"

Each time he yells, he readjusts the traffic cone on his head, like a bride fixing her veil in front of a mirror on her wedding day.

"Shortcut?" I suggest, and we enter the local high school grounds.

Jared and Drew make a beeline for a construction zone within the school. One of the wings is in the midst of extensive renovations. Temporary fences, machinery and workers huts line the buildings.

Drew picks up a TV and hurls it into the skip bin. *Smash!*

I look at the buildings and think back to how torturous school life had been the year before. My mind flickers through a series of detentions, strict rules, and bullying at the hands of students and teachers alike. I glance at the scars on my arm and ponder the possible connections between my chronic low self-esteem and the very grounds I'm standing in.

"Fuck it" I help myself to a long plank of wood and hurl it into the skip bin. Drew smiles.

"Fuck this place" says Jared, as he removes his new hat and throws it in the bin.

I gather scaffolding and foam that are lying around and throw them in too. Within minutes, the skip is piled high and overflowing with building materials. The surrounding area looks too immaculate for a construction zone. I pull out my cigarette lighter and ignite various parts of the overhanging objects.

"Whoa" Jared says.

Our faces are illuminated by the flames. The fire quickly engulfs the bin. Drew adds a few more boards to the blaze. *Whoosh!* The flames leap into the night sky and quickly reach the height of the second story buildings. We stand in awe at our creation and the power of the fire.

"Better get going" I say, noticing how the fire is spreading out of control and growing closer to the school buildings. We exit through the carpark.

"Why are you stopping?" Drew asks.

I remove a spray can from under my shirt that I found in the construction area. I stand in front of a small sign. It reads *PRINCIPAL.* I shake the can and position it over the sign. I spray *C-U-N-T* and nod with satisfaction.

I arrive home a short time later and gaze out the living room window. A large red glow beams up from the local high school.

***

"The lord is my shepherd; I shall not want. He maketh me to lie down in green pastures."

"Very green" Drew laughs. "Just roll the thing."

"Well, I figure we should read a line before we smoke it" I smirk.

We pass the joint around while intermittently coughing.

"Jared's mum has good weed" I gasp. "What is this stuff?"

"I don't know. Mum buys the stuff online and grows it in there" he says, pointing to a bright glow beneath the door.

"I thought you said that was the toilet" I say.

"It is" Jared sighs.

I turn my head to speak to Drew and everything rapidly turns slow-motion. My legs disconnect from the rest of my body.

"What did we smoke?" I say, slowly slithering off the couch into a puddle on the floor. "This carpet feels like a water bed."

Drew starts laughing like a cartoon chipmunk that just discovered a year's supply of nuts.

"It feels like I'm swimming" I say, slowly flapping my arms and legs around like I'm making a snow angel on his floor.

"Careful!" Jared says.

My arms and legs flail around and knock into tables and chairs.

"You're making too much noise!" Jared stresses. "You need to leave before mum hears."

Drew can't stop laughing and now appears like a chipmunk having a seizure.

"Out!" Jared demands.

We stumble into the night.

"Do you think it feels like we're walking in the stars?" I ask, pointing to the reflection of streetlights sparkling across the wet road.

"Remember that time we burned Jared's hat?" Drew replies, fashioning a traffic cone on his head.

"Loose surface" I reply, and attempt to lift an oversize traffic sign under my arm.

Drew places the traffic cone over his crotch and pretends to fire cannon balls from it.

A white panel van seemingly lights up in the distance. It looks cosy sitting there by itself. It appears innocent; unlike the menacing van filled with assailants from weeks earlier. I pull the door handle. It's unlocked.

"What are you doing?" Drew asks.

I sit in the driver seat, place my hands on the steering wheel and pretend to drive. *"Vroom!"* I open the glove compartment. I search through the contents, though not sure what I'm looking for, or what I will do if I find it. I close the glovebox, shut the car door and pick up my sign.

We walk around the corner and hear a car in the distance. We drop our traffic memorabilia and attempt to act casual, though our uneven gait gives us away. Our faces light up under a high beam. *Shit.* We start running. The car wheels screech and the engine revs loudly. I lose sight of Drew. The slow-motion feeling returns. My legs spin but I feel like a cartoon character going nowhere. I run onto the road. The car follows. It increases speed.

"Come here you little cunt!" yells a man from the car.

My feet loudly slap against the tarmac and my breathing becomes rapid. I realize I'm no Usain Bolt and can't outrun a car. I dart up the driveway of the closest house and turn the corner.

Internal fence. *Fuck.*

There is nowhere to go. The fence is too high. I'm cornered. I crouch in the shadows beside the house and lose balance. I crash into a metal trashcan that falls against the concrete, making a loud noise.

"We're gonna fucken stab you!" yells the car.

I curl up in a ball and attempt to muffle my breathing. An outside light turns on as a resident of the house searches for the origin of noise.

"Who is there?" he asks, shining a flashlight.

I wait for the flashlight to find me, like an escaped convict awaiting search lights to recapture him. I've pushed my luck too far. There is no escape this time. I shouldn't have smoked that bible, or opened that van door, or catapulted that possum, or started that fire, or stressed that Subway employee.

I look towards the side of the house. I wait for the people in the car to run around the corner with their knives and end it all.

I hear running footsteps and lower my head.

Drew.

I pull him down with me and place my hand over his mouth.

"Shut up" I whisper.

The car's engine continues to rev as it circles the block. "Come out you little cunts! We have a surprise for you!" they yell.

My heart races. We wait, and wait.

The stabbing somehow never comes. The car eventually drives away. The resident of the house mumbles something like "must be cats" and returns inside. An eternity passes and I gradually harness enough bravery to emerge from my corner. I expect to be jumped at any moment. But it never comes.

I arrive home safely and get into bed. I reach across my nightstand and grab the funeral program of my grandfather from the week before.

"I'm sorry" I cry. "I'll do better."

- *Rowan MacDonald*

The Girl You Wanted

At her father's funerary mass, Ruby took two knives from the church kitchen and drove them into the front tires of her ex-boyfriend's car.

It wasn't like Ruby wasn't raised with love and goodness— it wasn't like Ruby didn't know the difference between right and wrong. But she didn't regret what she did to Caleb's car, she just regretted not grabbing more knives.

"Ruby, you can't—" Her mom sighed, looking over at Ruby in the passenger seat. "You can't go around doing stuff like this."

Ruby bit her lip, staring at her own reflection in the side mirror of the car. Her mom reached over and brushed Ruby's hair behind her ear. "You know better than this."

Ruby's heart hurt. She wanted to rip it out of her. She wanted to scream it out of her. The knives had been a start, but they hadn't been enough. How could Caleb react so nonchalantly when she caught him with his hands and lips all over Ava at the funeral—and all Ruby wanted to do was to stab him?

"I know he hurt you." Her mother sighed. "But we don't take our anger out like that. We talk about it, okay?"

Ruby nodded.

"No more of this, okay?"

Ruby nodded.

At home, in her room, Ruby abandoned her journal beneath medicine bottles, discarded photos of her boyfriend and friends, a box of condoms, homework assignments, and dried roses she had bought for herself when Caleb hadn't seen the point in buying flowers. She didn't want to write, she didn't want to talk, she wanted to act. For a second, the burning she felt in her chest had almost glimmered to ashes when she punctured the tires and saw Caleb react back to her.

She wanted to make Caleb feel an ounce of what she felt—she wanted to make him cry the way he made her cry, she wanted to make him question himself the way he made her question herself. Ruby knew it would never be the same, she didn't have the emotional upper hand, but that didn't mean she had nothing.

***

With new scissors clutched in her hand, Ruby headed to the glue aisle. The days were blurring together, and had been so for weeks. Her mother had dropped her off at the art store to make posters for the upcoming Lunar New Year, or Tết, celebration while she went to the grocery store to stock up on pandan waffle ingredients. It was supposed to be a distraction.

"Hey Ruby."

Her hand stopped midair, an inch away from the glue. She glanced to the side and upon recognizing Aaron Nguyen, chose not to respond.

Ruby and Aaron's mothers were childhood friends, and they had tried to force that same fate onto their children to no avail. Ruby and Aaron had run in different crowds from the beginning. With the other girls, Ruby participated in Angel Dances for the Christmas Play or Fashion Shows for Tết. With the other boys, Aaron dicked around in the church parking lot, or back alley, or wherever they pleased.

"Are you okay?" he asked, his voice light. "I'm sorry about your dad. And I'm sorry about Caleb..."

Ruby responded, "Leave me alone."

The worst thing Aaron ever did was break up with his girlfriend when he was eighteen years old. Everybody at church called her the sweetest girl they ever knew, and everybody was pissed off when Aaron decided he didn't love her enough to go long distance with her. The worst part was that he did it right before she left the state, after they had spent the summer talking about forever.

Ruby was sixteen at the time, still friends with all the girls at church. She heard all the gossip flying around about him:

"He really just used her until the end."

"He's heartless for doing that to her."

"She treated him too well to be broken up with like that."

Ruby remembered he was grumpy about it one Sunday evening during their usual joint family dinners, only a few weeks after the horribly public break-up. Ruby told him, "You weren't wrong for being honest." But his honesty now was insufferable.

"It was shitty of him," Aaron went on. "For him to date you when he liked someone else—"

Ruby spun on her heel and walked away, but Aaron was insistent.

"I'm sorry, I shouldn't have said that, huh?"

"Fuck off, Aaron."

"Hey—aren't we friends?" he asked her.

"What gave you that idea?" she snapped.

"You said—"

Through all their family dinners, family vacations, and random church events, their friendship was a here-and-there kind of thing. She remembered the conversation she had with Aaron at one of Caleb's parties. She almost fell over from the heady mix of alcohol and jumping around too much when Aaron had caught her. She remembered squishing his cheeks, saying, "You're such a good friend." Boys were so simple.

"You can fuck off, and you can tell Caleb to fuck off too," she said.

Aaron frowned.

"And I forgot my glue, damn it."

"I don't know why you're mad at me, I didn't do anything to you," he said back, his voice just as harsh.

"Like you're not going to text Caleb after this and bitch about me." She scowled. "All you and everybody at church wants to know is how I feel about Caleb so you can report back to him, but I'm not telling anyone anything anymore."

"I'm not going to tell Caleb—I just—I'm worried about you. Nobody has seen you for two weeks. Not after…"

The tire slashing incident.

"So? Leave me alone unless you want to be next."

He sighed. "Fine, whatever, bye."

She stood still as he went away, and an idea came to her. As he turned the corner into the paint section, she found herself following him. He perused the canvases, and she stomped down to meet him in the middle of the aisle.

He frowned, giving her a quizzical look. She grabbed him by the collar of his jacket and pressed a hasty kiss to his lips. The canvas clattered to the ground. His hands found their way into her hair, but it didn't last long before he pulled away.

"What—" he began.

"Bye."

"Ruby—"

"Call me."

"Why—" he said, but Ruby rounded the corner, her heartbeat like thunder in her ear.

***

When Aaron's grandparents on his mom's side passed away, Ruby's mom— Cô Thuy—brought food over for an entire month. Now, in Cô Thuy's time of need, his mom was returning the favor.

His mom and Cô Thuy were talking up a storm about Ruby and her current behavior, but all Aaron could focus on was how pristine and modern the house appeared. He had been here a thousand times, but for the past month the family dinners had been held at Aaron's house because of the Huynh's kitchen renovations.

The cupboards were all glass, giving open views to the neatly stacked white porcelain plates and bowls, glass cups, and ceramic mugs. All the spices were labeled prettily. All the snacks were sorted into clear bins instead of their original casings. All of the utensils were stacked on top of each other, not just shoved in the drawer the way they were at his house. All the knives were hanging on a magnetic strip on the wall by the counter. Their fridge was another level of organization—with a separate freezer for a variety of ice cream and a separate fridge for drinks of various brands.

Even the house layout was open space. From where he sat in the kitchen, he could see into the foyer, and past the foyer into the dining room. Everything was so visible. For someone who lived in a house that didn't have any secrets, Ruby was strangely mysterious.

"I don't know what to do with her," Cô Thuy whispered. "She worries me more and more every day. I know we've both been struggling since he died…but it's more than that for her…"

"Heartbreak is one of the worst things a girl can go through," Aaron's mom murmured.

"She lost her dad and her boyfriend, she just needs to cry."

"But she's not crying."

"She needs time, and help." Aaron's mom nodded. "Maybe she should talk to Cha. He gave me good advice when—"

Aaron highly doubted talking to their sixty-year-old priest would help anything.

The front door swung open, and the two mothers quieted, plastering on smiles as Ruby walked in. She stopped when she saw Aaron.

"Con chào Cô Hien," Ruby greeted Aaron's mom. Then to her mom, she said, "I'm going to my room."

"Cô brought dinner," Cô Thuy said. "Come have some."

"I'm not hungry."

"We can go for ice cream," Aaron suddenly suggested. "You like ice cream, right?"

Ruby stilled at the bottom of the staircase. Everybody seemed to hold their breath. Aaron half expected her to ignore him and go upstairs, but she met his gaze and said, "Okay."

In his car, he told himself that they were just going to talk, repeated like a mantra that she needed a friend, reminded himself to be nice and ask about her dad or about Caleb or about how she was dealing with the grief. The kiss had been a mistake, he decided.

Her jacket shifted off of her shoulders, revealing a tiny cropped tank top, the black spaghetti string falling wayside along with her jacket. He wondered if she was cold and why she hadn't zipped up her jacket—or had she unzipped it in the car? And she leaned across the center console.

"I don't want ice cream," she said.

"Okay, what did you want then?"

"Drive to the park."

"Why?"

"Just do it."

The only light was the streetlamp outside of the window, but Aaron could see her face blooming red. Was she nervous? Why did she keep getting closer? She pressed her chest against his arm.

"Are you…" His voice faltered as she looked into his eyes. He couldn't move. He didn't want to touch her, he wanted to touch her. He coughed, "How are you?"

"I'm sad."

"Really?"

"You should make me feel better."

"Do you wanna talk about—"

"Shut up," she said, pulling him in by his collar again.

In the backseat of his car, he pulled her onto him.

He never looked at her before this, but he was looking at her now. His hands found their way into her hair, tilting her head back to show more of her neck, like there wasn't enough skin to work with already. The way her breath caught when he bit her excited him even more. Her shaky hands cupped his face so gently, and he wondered how she could be so innocent.

His hands slipped under her shirt, fingertips tracing her ribs, going up, up, up. When Ruby pulled away, Aaron almost apologized, but she pulled her shirt off instead. She ran a hand through her short hair, her pale skin in the dim light lured him in even more. She looked so untouched. Aaron brushed a stray strand of hair behind her ear, and then pulled her back in for a kiss. Her hands clumsily fumbled at his jeans.

"Wait," he murmured against her, stopping her hands. "Slow down— are you sure—"

Her face was hidden as she pressed a soft kiss against his cheek and then his ear, she whispered, "I just want you inside of me."

That was enough of an invitation.

Afterwards, they sat quietly in their respective seats in the front.

"Do you feel better?" Aaron mused, starting the car.

She laughed. "Yes."

***

The scissors and glitter glue were meant for Tết posters, but Ruby took them to Caleb's house instead. It was a warm Sunday afternoon for a February. Everybody was still out at brunch or running errands or visiting family or, in Caleb's case, still at church, hanging all over Ava. She stared up at Caleb's window, the window she had climbed through so many times at night for his benefit. He always left it unlocked.

Ruby had begun to doubt her own villainy. She dreamed of revenge, but making the posters had calmed her down a little. But when she brought

72

the posters to church, Ava leaned over, put a hand on Ruby's wrist, and said, "Thanks, but I'm actually printing posters, so you can take these home."

Ruby ripped her hands away from Ava. It wasn't about the posters.

Ava then said, "Oh, you're not still upset about Caleb, right? He's always liked me, you knew that. I'm not saying what happened was right, but it was just a mistake. I would never hurt you on purpose, Ruby."

I don't like her, I like you. What pretty lies Caleb had whispered in her ear.

Every cell in her burned up when she used to watch Ava touch Caleb's hand or chest, laughing at all the things he said, taking up the space beside him during church meetings or while at lunch. Ruby had known they were close friends, but this was too close for comfort. Her mother had told her never to make a scene, that it wasn't worth it, that it was better to hold it in and let it out in private where nobody could judge. So Ruby suffered it in public.

But when Ruby and Caleb were alone, the questions flooded out:

"Do you like her?"

"Why does it feel like she's flirting with you?"

"Can you tell her to stop?"

"Can you not flirt back with her?"

"Does she like you?"

"Can you just be honest with me?"

Ruby asked, and asked, and asked. She didn't know what else to do. Caleb answered:

"She's not flirting with me, it's just her personality."

"We're just friends, Ruby, don't worry about it."

"Can you stop being paranoid? We've always been like this with each other."

"I'm not lying to you, Ruby! Stop making me feel bad when I'm telling you everything already."

I like you, Ruby. I like you, Ruby. I like you, Ruby.

She had been played for a fool. Everybody at church had whispered and giggled about Ava and Caleb right in front of Ruby, and acted dumb when she tried to find out the truth.

Apparently it wasn't their secret to tell her.

Every lie Caleb told about Ava replayed itself in her head until she was shaking, her fingertips digging into the palm of her hands until she drew blood, her teeth gnawing into her bottom lip until she bled. Seeing his hurt when she wrecked his car was nice, but she needed more.

In Caleb's room, Ruby set to work. She cut up his blankets and sheets and pillows, the place she had laid with him so many times, let him use her so many times, so mindlessly convinced that she could keep his attention if she just gave in to everything he wanted. She had never minded the lack of pleasure she felt from blowing him if it meant he looked at her like she was sent from heaven, if it meant she was doing something right.

Then she found his clothes and shoes. She tore her scissors through any fabric she could find and poured glitter glue all over the precious tennis shoes he had spent so much money on.

He had prided himself so much on his street apparel and teased Ruby for looking so preppy. All Ruby could see now was that he was tearing her down, to make her into nothing. Now he would be nothing too.

Then there were his Xbox games. So many times he had excused his lack of response on games, maybe he had been playing games, but Ruby was beginning to suspect that more than half those times were actually spent with Ava. She opened each box and snapped the discs in half. She even squeezed glitter glue into the DVD slot of his Xbox, determined to make his life impossible to live.

Ruby stood in the ruination afterward and realized her own mistake. While the anger in her chest had dissipated, she couldn't relax.

***

Aaron stared at the empty seat across from him where Ruby usually sat at dinner. At their past family dinners, he and Ruby would say hi, ask each other about school, and never go past formalities. Sometimes they quietly smiled and laughed as they listened to their moms try to parse teenage slang or talk about politics. Most of the time, Aaron would eat dinner and then sit on the couch scrolling through his phone or doing homework until his mom was done talking. He never minded the Sundays in the Huynh house because it was one Sunday a month, and he got good food out of it too.

Things seemed to return to normal. Aaron went about his daily routine. His mom cooked less for the Huynh's. Ruby was finally back in school, though she wasn't attending church anymore. Cô Thuy spoke about working and sorting through her late husband's affairs.

But family dinners were disrupted. Ruby was never home. Sometimes, Ruby had been with him, but most of the time, she was out and about, and missed calls and didn't answer text messages. Aaron wondered if she would ever actually let him take her out for ice cream—but she always ended up kissing him, and he would get so drunk on her that he forgot his first objective. Nights with Ruby were different from dinners at her house. It was like she came alive in the dark. She didn't talk more, but she moved and acted with a confidence he didn't know she possessed. She asked for what she wanted with no words at all. He wondered if she understood him that well, or maybe he understood her that well—either way, their nights together were like fever dreams.

Aaron swirled his chopsticks in the pho broth, and the moms' conversation was interrupted by Cô Thuy's phone ringing. Cô Thuy took the call and froze. She apologized profusely to the caller and said she would deal with Ruby as soon as possible. Then she dialed Ruby, who promptly ended the call without even giving the phone a chance to ring. Just like that, dinner was cut short.

At home, Aaron tried to think of a casual text he could send Ruby to figure out what happened when a knock on the door interrupted him. Caleb pushed past Aaron, kicked off his shoes, and stomped into the kitchen, taking a beer from the fridge. Aaron quickly grabbed the glass bottle from his hand and said, "Dude, my mom's home."

"Like she cares."

"Well, she'll notice if this is gone," Aaron said, putting the drink back. "What are you doing here?"

"You know she's just messing with you, right?" Caleb changed the subject. "She's just ho-ing around because she's bitter."

"What?" Aaron asked.

"Ruby? She's a ho, and she's using you," Caleb sneered. "I know about you and Ruby. Why are you hiding it?"

"I wasn't hiding it," Aaron shrugged. "I just—I never talk about this shit with you. We never talk about this shit."

"Well, maybe you should've talked to me because she's my ex."

"You dumped her," Aaron argued. "Actually, you cheated on her for months, and then she left you, but you told everyone that—God, none of that matters, why do you care? Aren't you with Ava now?"

Caleb stared at Aaron with such a confused look of contempt. It was like Caleb didn't even know what had come over himself. Caleb took a deep breath. "Sorry, man, I don't know what's wrong with me. I just—Ruby's fucking with me."

"What?"

"Ruby. She fucked up my car and now she destroyed my room, Aaron. I came home today and everything was ripped up and broken. Like you just have to see for yourself."

Aaron took a deep breath, "Whoa."

Caleb leaned back against the kitchen table and looked Aaron in the eyes, defeat evident in his eyes as he said, "And then I hear from Ava that you and Ruby are sleeping with each other? I don't know—I haven't seen Ruby in weeks, but it feels like she's fucking with my head."

Aaron didn't know what to say.

Caleb crossed his arms, "Dude, just don't fuck with Ruby 'cause she's my ex and she's psycho."

***

Aaron knocked on the door of the Huynh's house. When Ruby opened the door, he faltered, taking in her blotchy face, messy hair pulled into a low ponytail, and her dead stare.

"I'm not hungry."

"Ruby, are you okay?"

In response, she tried to shut the door on him.

"Ruby." He stopped the door with his foot. "Come on, let me in."

In the kitchen, he sat down at the island while she lounged by the stove. He could see through everything in the kitchen but her. If only she would look him in the eyes and tell him what was wrong. But she just went upstairs. He followed.

Aaron had never been in Ruby's room. Her bed was unmade. Clothes, dead flowers, loose condoms, random notebooks and books, and shredded pictures were strewn across the floor, desk, and nightstand. A picture of her and her parents stood beside a broken glass cup and a packet of pills—maybe birth control, he wasn't sure. He wondered why she hadn't cleaned up the broken glass yet. He wanted to clean it for her.

Ruby pulled off her sweater and shimmied off her sweatpants. To protect her dignity,

Aaron turned his back and shut the door. "What are you doing—"

"Kiss me," Ruby said, wrapping her arms around him.

"Ruby." Aaron pulled out of her embrace and faced her. "No. This isn't a good idea."

"This is what you want from me, isn't it?" Ruby accused.

"What? No. I want you to talk to me."

"Well, I don't want to talk, so fuck me or leave," Ruby snapped.

She had always been thin, but her skin was beginning to sink into her bones. In the dark, every time he touched her hip or collarbone, she felt sharp enough to cut. In the light, all he could see was her body wasting away.

He held her by the shoulders, her skin cold in his hands.

"I'm worried about you. We're all worried about you."

"You don't even know me," Ruby sneered.

"We've known each other all our lives."

"Yeah, but you don't know me. Don't act like you care about me."

"Ruby, I love you even when there are times I don't like you," Aaron said.

Ruby shrugged Aaron's hands off of her shoulders. "You love me? But you don't like me?"

"I know what you did to Caleb's room. I know you're mad at him, but aren't you doing too much?"

"Too much?" Ruby scoffed.

He moved past her, grabbed a blanket from her bed, and wrapped it around her shoulders.

"What do you know, Aaron?" she demanded, her voice scorching. "Did you know about the other girls? Did you know about Caleb and Ava? Do you think all of Caleb's lies were too much?"

Aaron didn't know the details of her relationship with Caleb, but Caleb had always been friendly with other girls, and even more so with Ava. But it wasn't Aaron's job to keep a tab on what Caleb was doing. That was Caleb's life, not his.

"I'm not saying he's right," Aaron backtracked. "I just—I think you're better than how you're acting now."

He didn't know what he was trying to say or what Ruby wanted to hear. But Ava and Caleb—while what they did wasn't right, it was a mistake, a moment of weakness in attraction. Mistakes happened with how flirtatious Caleb and Ava were. But Ruby? She wasn't violent or angry or so horrible—she was quiet, demure, unassuming. She wasn't acting like herself.

But Ruby asked, "What if I'm just like this? What if everything I did to Caleb is just a mistake I made?"

Aaron shook his head, "You're not like this. You're better than this, Ruby."

"Why aren't Caleb and Ava better than their mistakes?" Ruby whispered.

Aaron shook his head, "You're missing the point—"

"Get out, Aaron."

"Ruby."

"I already told you—if you're not going to fuck me, just leave," she said. She began to pull her clothes back on, and the silence between them stretched on until Aaron decided to leave.

"At least eat," he whispered.

***

Ruby turned her dad's keychain over in her hand. She didn't know how to drive, she never learned. The unknown of driving filled her with fear. Her mother rolled her eyes, but her dad told her he would drive her until she absolutely had to get her own car.

Her dad had been on his way to pick her up from school for the weekend when a car running a red light hit him at the intersection. Her dad was usually the one who had the penchant for speeding through just as the light turned red, and it scared the Hell out of Ruby and her mom. But he laughed and said they'd never get hurt as long as he was the one driving. Then her mom would recall the story she had told a thousand times about how they got into a motorcycle accident back in Vietnam because of his recklessness. But they both laughed it off because near death experiences made for some of the most romantic stories.

The day of his accident, Ruby and her mom sped to the hospital only to find a body. The last thing her mom had said to him was "bye". The last thing he had said to Ruby was, "See you soon", and Ruby answered, "Okay", before hanging up. She should've said, "I love you", but they rarely said things like that in their family—not unless someone was dying. Ruby turned her dad's keychain over in her hand. She ran her hand over the bent metal.

She remembered when anything and everything moved her to tears— someone pushed her, she scraped her knees, she couldn't get a cadence right in her piano piece, her mom yelled at her, or her dad wasn't listening to her. If something was even a little wrong, Ruby cried and cried until her head hurt and she threw up.

One of the last times she fell into a crying spell, her mom rubbed Ruby's face dry, cupped it in her hands, and said, "Sometimes you scare me."

Ruby was nine, and didn't know what to make of the words. But her mom didn't mince her words with the next lecture: "You're a big girl now, Ruby. You can't cry like a baby anymore. You have to solve your problems. So whenever you feel like crying, chant to yourself 'don't cry, don't cry, don't cry', and take a deep breath."

For a while it worked. Her mom was pleased with her controlled emotions. But there were days Ruby felt like she would burst into flames. She would rush out of the house, unable to breath, thinking she was going to die. She didn't know what it was—some kind of upset that made Ruby feel so much she couldn't fathom how anybody could keep themselves together. If her dad found her, he would put a glass of water into her hands, and ask for her help with something around the house.

Ruby turned her dad's keychain over in her hand. She wanted to cry now, but if she started, she wouldn't stop.

Her bedroom door creaked open. "Did you go to church today?" her mother asked, as she came to Ruby's bedside.

Ruby shook her head.

Her mother patted her arm. "Please, go. God will help us."

Ruby nodded.

Platitudes could go to Hell. Words meant nothing to her anymore.

Her mother brushed the hairs off Ruby's face. "Ruby, if you ever need to talk, I'm here, Cô Hien is here, Aaron is here, Cha is here, God is here. We're all here for you. But please, you need to stop acting this way. You've always been gentle, loving, and good. I taught you better than this, I taught you to be good. You can't hurt people like this."

Ruby clutched her dad's keychain so tightly that the edges dug into the palm of her hand.

"Can't you be good for me?" her mother whispered. "Because I—I— can't do this alone…and your dad wouldn't want you doing this either."

Her mother's words and tears burned Ruby. She hadn't been loved when she was good. And she couldn't be loved if she was bad.

***

Ruby watched as the red and gold lions danced around the basement of the church, collecting donations from kids and parents for Tết. She remembered bursting into tears as a child when the lions came up to her, and her father hugging her tight as he chuckled at her reaction. Now, she stood on the sidelines waiting for all of this to pass. She wanted to be anywhere but home or church. But here she was anyway, for her mom, to make her mom believe she was okay. Ruby was trying.

But the sight of Ava fluttering past with her group of friends, giggling and chattering about the couple's fashion show for Tết broke something in Ruby. Again. Every single time. Ava's life returned to normal after she tore her way through Ruby and Caleb's relationship—but Ruby felt like every bone in her body was broken. Her eyes followed Ava. Ava flipped her long, curly hair over her shoulder. Ava's laugh rang through the room right before she disappeared around the corner with her friends into the waiting room. But the sound lingered. Ruby hated even more the sea of comments around her—

"Ava looks so pretty today."

"She's the nicest, she helped make the poster for Tết this year, did you know?"

"She's so talented!"

Ava this, Ava that—no wonder Caleb wanted Ava more than her. But no, that wasn't the whole story, Ava had also wanted Caleb.

In the waiting room, the fluttering and fretting of all the girls brought Ruby back to a time when she was a part of this circle. Dressed in pretty clothes, the fabric flowing around the room, straw hats being handed around in chaotic order, giggling with her girlfriends, one of whom used to be Ava. Ruby had never been the center of attention the way Ava was now, but that made it all the easier.

She found a pair of mislaid scissors on the counter.

Hands were all over Ava already, fixing her hair, helping straightening out her ao dai, and others trying to touch-up her makeup.

The soft fabric felt foreign in Ruby's hands, and the scissors began to snip, snip, snip. Someone screamed. Ava jerked. The scissors tore the thin fabric. Ava screamed. Ruby pulled the scissors away, but they went right back

79

to their original task, and found their way into Ava's hair. Ava raised her hands to block the attack—when a hand closed around Ruby's wrist.

Aaron lowered the bloody scissors. "Ruby. Stop."

The scissors clattered to the ground. Ava's torn dress, uneven hair, and bloody hand flooded Ruby's vision. Ava's blood stained Ruby's hand, and bile rose in Ruby's throat. She pressed her clean hand to her mouth and ran out of the room.

She managed to keep from throwing up from the sight of blood, but she was beginning to shake as she rubbed Ava's blood into the snow. Ava was such a tangible extension of Caleb. Ruby had imagined this revenge against Caleb, against Ava, but she hadn't imagined drawing blood until it happened. Aaron followed her, and he wrapped his jacket around her shoulders.

"I have to go," Ruby whispered, staring at the stained snow.

"No, you have to apologize."

It was the right thing, the good thing, the only thing she could do to make herself look sane. But it wasn't honest.

"Yeah fucking right." Ruby tossed his jacket back to him.

"Ruby," he yelled, as she stormed away. "This isn't you—you're not acting like yourself, you're acting crazy—"

Aaron's so-called care suffocated Ruby. The nights he kissed her forehead and held her so close it almost scared her to the point of tears. The care had felt real, but he should've just stayed a pawn in her game or a late-night hookup. He didn't care. Remembering that hurt more.

***

There were flowers in Aaron's hands and a boy in Ruby's bed. Ruby had told Aaron in passing once that Caleb never bought her flowers. Aaron, in an effort to soothe Ruby's emotions and persuade her to be more reasonable, bought her pretty, white daisies. He assumed they would match her sensibilities. But Ruby had a different boy in her bed.

Ruby stared at the flowers. "Huh."

Aaron turned on his heel and marched out of the house.

Ruby called after him, "We're not dating, Aaron."

"I can see that," he snapped back. "You're just ho-ing around, aren't you? Caleb was right—you're just—" He took a deep breath, staring at Ruby from down the hallway. "I liked you. I told you I liked you."

"But what do you like about me?" Ruby asked, her voice bitter. "You don't know the first thing about me. You probably just like the way I suck your dick."

That girl he knew from childhood was not the girl standing before him now. She had changed, but how? What did he like about her? He hadn't liked

80

her before. She had been too quiet back then. Did he even like her now? She was still quiet. He tried to find something that wasn't physical, but all he could think about was running his hands through her soft, silky hair, her pink lips on his neck, reaching up to caress her while she rode him, and her soft gasp when he bit her chest too hard but she liked it when it hurt a little.

He didn't like her. He hated that she was right.

He met her gaze, and her eyes burned into him. He tossed the flowers on the ground, and left the house.

Her careless behavior cut him to the bone. He hadn't believed her to be capable of such ruthlessness, that everything she had done up to this point was not the real Ruby. But he had assumed everything about her, made believe she was a doe-eyed girl with tears in her eyes, measured in every aspect of her life, and ready to please. Aaron had only wanted her to be that way.

***

There was something painful about the human body. The needle hanging out of Ruby's arm, drawing out blood by what seemed like the gallon, didn't help the case.

"What grade are you in?" the nurse asked, a distraction of sorts.

"I'm a freshman, in college," she murmured, her eyes still squeezed shut.

"What are you studying?"

"I don't know yet."

"Most people don't. What are you interested in?"

"Um…I don't know. A lot of things. Not science, I hate science. I hate…blood."

"It's almost done, sweetie."

The worst thing about STI tests were the blood tests, and Ruby tried to avoid it at all costs, but after everything with Aaron, sex hurt. Every touch, every kiss, every look. She felt sick to her stomach every time she saw the flowers Aaron brought her. She didn't have it in her to throw them away—they were the first flowers a boy ever gave her.

She hated the human body. Everything hurt, with or without a reason.

"You're done now. Do you want some juice?"

"Yes, please."

The cold apple juice soothed the pain, but that lasted only as long as she had juice.

"You're free to go when you're ready," the nurse said.

She walked home, her body numb from the cold.

"Where have you been?" her mother demanded when she came through the door.

81

"Out."

"Ruby, you can't just be running off like this."

"Okay," she said.

But her mother crossed her arms, her voice shaking, "Ruby, we need to talk."

"About what?"

"About your behavior. This isn't you, and you need help."

All anybody ever wanted from her was for her to sit still, be quiet, smile pleasantly. She closed her eyes.

"Okay."

Ruby's mom breathed, "I want you to go to therapy. I—I want you to try it."

"Okay."

Ruby's mom wrapped her into a hug. "I just want you back."

The Ruby everybody wanted back was dead and gone. Ruby had burned that girl to ashes a long time ago, and she would never let herself be so malleable and easily manipulated.

Ruby's mom let out a shaky breath. "Okay. I'm going to cook dinner. Cô Hien and Aaron will be over tonight. You'll join us, won't you? Please, Ruby?"

Ruby looked at the ground. "Okay."

Her mom went back to the kitchen.

Caleb never liked her. Ava played her like a fool. Ruby's mom wanted her to be sweet and quiet and good. Aaron hated her now. She wanted to stop existing in other people's lives as their playthings or problems. Every hookup was the closest thing she could get to being nothing, because it meant nothing to those boys and nothing to her. But here in her house and in her life and in her little community of lies and secrets, she was a puppet on a string, dancing when people wanted her to dance, disappearing when people wanted her to disappear.

***

Aaron walked into the Huynh's house, prepared to ignore Ruby through dinner, but all he heard was frantic crying. His mom didn't bother taking off her boots as she rushed into the kitchen and pulled Cô Thuy into her arms, begging to know what was wrong.

"Ruby—she took my car," Cô Thuy cried. "She doesn't even know how to drive. I don't know who to call—I don't know what to do—I thought, I thought—I tried talking to her, to get her help, and I thought—"

Aaron's mom stroked Cô Thuy's hair, "Shhh, shhh, shhh, it's okay. It's okay. Ruby will be okay."

"I just want Ruby back," Cô Thuy cried.

If she had been the girl she was two years ago, she would've slipped away. Her story, her part in the world, her life minimized to a side plot in a greater story. Ruby's outrage was an effort to make people look, to make people see her, no matter how ugly she acted—and all anybody ever wanted was for her to go quietly. Aaron could count on both hands the chances he had to see Ruby for the person she was becoming—but each time, he brushed her under the rug like everybody else.

***

As she drove, Ruby's thoughts and feelings caught up to her. She didn't know what she wanted or needed from anyone. But she knew what she didn't want— to go back to being the old Ruby. That girl trusted too easily, smiled without meaning it, believed everybody around her was good. She had tried so hard to understand them she barely understood herself. Everybody she used to think was important took up space inside of her, and she didn't know who she was beyond what they wanted—for her to be good.

But she couldn't be good anymore. She couldn't keep pleasing everyone without feeling wrong inside. She could only be the girl they wanted if she stopped feeling so much. Her mom was already right about everybody at their church community. Maybe her mom was also right about her dad—if he was here, maybe he'd scold her, too, be scared of her too.

Foot on the pedal, hands clenched around the steering wheel, she blinked away tears, prayed for everything around her to stop, and missed the red light in front of her.

- Anna Chu

The Mulch

As air last rasps sufferance,
Hunger leads us
To the mulch.

And I, a guilt-struck animal,
Snared and in shock,
My actions form my life
In vivifying rust.

Yet today I count grain,
Fingers thinning
Through tilling
Millimetres
Of brittle kernels.

And my heart fills
To the forgotten sound
Of moorland birds.

And in lieu of breath,
I exhale clouds
Of butterflies.

- Oisin Breen

The System

We tried to run the system—
The way we'd been taught—
But it just wouldn't work,
No matter what we did.
We consulted the latest manual—
In, at least, nine languages—
Phoned a support hotline,
Scheduled an expensive home visit,
Yet, utterly, to no avail.
We were at our wits' end.
If there was anything, whatsoever,
We'd been able to count on—
Year after year after year—
It was, certainly, the system,
And how, indeed, it represented
The state of the art,
In all its various manifestations,
Despite prevailing notions, regarding
A population hell-bent on change.
It was, then, with much misgiving,
We took it upon ourselves
To undo what was once done—
Dismantle the entire operation,
Until it simply failed to exist.
Even we couldn't recognize it,
After we made our final decision,
Sending it spinning into the heap.
Nowadays, there's a befitting silence,
Waiting to greet us each morning.
I guess it comes with the territory—
This end of the cycle,
As we well know it.

- Bart Edelman

What It Takes

So goddamn genteel—ladies,
with their voices always low
 and soothing like Cordelia's,
they're magnolia blossoms
and milk punch, their long blonde hair
tossed over the shoulder
with a flutter of eyelashes.

For sure I'll never drive
a white Jag convertible
like they've got,
or snag the smooth guy
with the private school accent
and barrels of money
so long as I keep saying
things like, "No shit!"

Here I am right now
absentmindedly swigging my beer
right out of the bottle
in the upstairs dining room
of the Dallas Museum of Art
even though they've given me
a lovely chilled glass.

- Lynn Gilbert

Regardless

As at every family gathering,
my mother, aunts, and grandmother
wallowed in concocted drama—

bruised feelings, misunderstood motives,
each woman bent on justifying herself
in the eyes of the others—but this time

Grandpa was coping alone
with his bone cancer and I, at fifteen
wanted to yell, *"The man's dying!*

Look at what's happening, for once!
See his hands washing each other,
his distant face, the clothes

hanging loose on him? Knock it off!
Who cares which doctor knows better

or whether he gets addicted
on his way to the grave?" But in this opera
they'd chosen all their own arias and

they sang them regardless.

- Lynn Gilbert

Trick Bag

Wojcik was sitting at the back of Ms. Goodwin's GED class today, bragging about killing a girl. She'd been holding out on him, he said, so he'd gone over to administer a beating, only the little Black heifer wouldn't shut her mouth, take what was coming to her.

I walked up behind him. "Shut yours, Wojcik."

"My remarks were not directed to you, Sergeant." His posse, weak little white guys, exchanged admiring glances at this.

"Mine are directed at you. Passed any tests yet?"

Ms. Goodwin came trotting. "The students work at their own pace here."

I looked at the empty table where Wojcik sat with his friends.

The Blacks and Hispanics were in front of a bank of computers set up on the opposite wall. No games, no music videos, just math problems.

Wojcik had been in the class for six months. Most of the offenders finish sooner. They need a high school diploma or a GED to get a prison job. Usually they want to work, for something to do and the forty cents an hour.

Wojcik has money. I've seen him in line at the commissary buying fried chicken and ice cream for his friends. Recruits, probably. Wojcik is a transfer from Illinois. They sent him to us because he'd been a shot caller for the Dirty White Boys there, appears to be working up to that here.

When we lined the offenders up in the salle port for the eleven o'clock gate the Black guys had fun with Wojcik.

"Sergeant's concerned about your lack of academic progress," Lamar Bean observed.

I was patting Wojcik down then, moving my hands over his chest. He sucked in a breath, let it out.

"Worried sick," someone agreed.

My officers laughed. Bad for discipline, but I grinned myself. Lamar is a pimp and a thief, shouldn't be so likeable.

The posse smoldered.

I was sitting at the officer's station when Ms. Goodwin came, leaned across the counter in a way I do not tolerate from offenders.

Stand two feet back and wait to be acknowledged before advancing.

I hated looking up, hated her hot breath in my face. I stood, giving her the full benefit of my height.

"I sensed you felt uncomfortable this morning, Sergeant."

I didn't answer.

She smiled. "Would it surprise you to learn what he said didn't bother me?"

He didn't kill you.

"I accept my students for who they are right now. That's why I don't jump on them for every little thing. Of course I know not everyone feels as I do. Perhaps you have a daughter?"

It's been a while since I got through a day without finding fault with Lorrie.

"Well, I'm sure you don't like to hear people speak disrespectfully about women," she said, when I didn't answer. "But if no one's been kind to you, how will you learn to be kind to others? Hence the music, the colorful posters, the parties. I want them to feel welcome."

Ms. Goodwin had one of her parties last week, didn't submit the paperwork to get it approved. I could hear the music, spread it, bitch, spread it, from my office.

Wojcik was standing at a table full of cookies and potato chips, pouring a liter bottle of Coke into Red Solo Cups.

The Blacks, I saw, kept to themselves.

Wojcik waved a cup at me. "Join us, Sergeant."

Oh, hence no.

I talked to Ms. Goodwin afterwards. The other teachers should have told her the way things are before Wojcik took over, but I never see her hanging out with them, standing around someone's desk, looking at shoes on the computer.

"You know how I am, Sergeant. I always forget the rules. And they're so important too."

I looked into her smug face, wanted to be shut of her.

She sighed. "Shall we agree to disagree?"

"This is policy. There's no room for disagreement."

I continued to stand as she stumped off.

The appropriate next step would be to bring Ms. Goodwin's classroom management to the attention of the school director, Kevin. He told me to call him that. His son Cody is a fifth grader in Lorrie's class, High Achievers, for gifted and talented third, fourth, and fifth graders. We'd gone to a potluck for the families last spring after Lorrie was accepted into the program. When Kevin saw me he expressed surprise, asked if Lorrie was adopted.

Let it go, my wife Lisa said afterwards. He meant to be funny.

Haha.

Anything I say, Kevin thinks it's a joke.

When it was time to get Lorrie today she wasn't at the pickup spot. I had to get out of the car to look for her. They're wasteful at her school, leave the sprinklers on overnight. Lorrie and some little boys were squishing through the marshy grass in back, splatting each other. She ran to me, daddy,

daddy, daddy, hugged my stomach. Even after she got her scolding for not being where she was supposed to be, she stayed bright, talked about wanting to do something special this afternoon.

"Guess what."

Her lacy tights were gray and damp from the water she'd kicked up. "Buy you something?" I shouldn't have said it. Lorrie knows better than to pester me for stuff.

"Funny daddy." She wanted to go to the park for buckeyes. She and Lisa use them for art projects. "The trees are so beautiful in the sunlight. Like lovely ladies dressed in gowns of red and yellow."

Mrs. Swenson must have read the boys and girls a poem about autumn.

I found her a bag in the glove compartment, waited for her on a bench by the car. Two young girls walking by, stopped to watch her stomping on the prickly green coverings to get out the buckeyes, smiled. Maybe they thought her enthusiasm was cute because Lorrie herself isn't cute, not as it's measured in little girls. When she came back, she was holding the skirt of her dress out in front of her, to carry the buckeyes. "I feel like a pioneer girl."

"Put them in the bag. That's what it's for."

When we got home she unzipped her backpack in the front hall and I saw the Olaf Beanie Baby, asked where it was from.

School. A prize for spelling.

Lorrie gets all kinds of trinkets, stickers, plastic junk, for reading books, completing online courses, good behavior. This was on a different level.

"That's a big prize."

"I think the PTA paid for it." This came so quickly I was sure she was lying. "Or maybe it was a special sale."

"Tell me where you got this, Lorrie. We need to give it back."

"I told you where I got it."

Inmates do that too, look hurt and bewildered when challenged.

"You're going to be punished. When your mother gets home she and I will decide how."

"Mommy will believe me." She might. She wouldn't care for my approach, that much I knew.

When Lorrie tried to walk past me, to the staircase, I held her shoulders, stooped to look in her face. "You cried your eyes out when you lost your mermaid doll last year. That's how you made someone feel, taking what isn't yours."

Lisa had wanted to get her another doll but I'd said no. We'd told Lorrie not to take toys to school. If she had to do without maybe she'd listen.

When I let go she walked upstairs, shut the door behind her.

Before she started High Achievers this year Lorrie was the only non-Hispanic child in a dual language program, kindergarten through second grade. Playing house, trucks, blocks, finger painting. The head teacher, Mr. Rubio, sang a welcome song to every child, every day. Well, good morning to Lorrie. Good morning to Lorrie. I'm glad to see you here! I thought it would put Lorrie at an academic disadvantage. But Lisa is a teacher herself and she said Mr. Rubio is the best there is.

"Performing well above grade level," he told us at every conference, "fluent in Spanish." When he'd show us her work I'd wonder when she'd found time to learn to read and write so well.

Lorrie loved it. "Guess who had fun today," she'd say when I picked her up.

She's the smartest child in High Achievers too. It must sting, being in trouble like an ordinary little girl.

I went to her door, said she could come out after she told me what had happened.

No answer.

I didn't want the school in my business but Mrs. Swenson might know who was missing an Olaf.

She answered my email at once, said Lorrie had won the all-school spelling bee that afternoon, the first third grader to win in school history. Olaf was a prize from the school treasure chest.

You can see what it looked like, I imagined myself telling Lisa.

I hadn't realized the Bee was today. Lorrie may have mentioned it this morning but I wasn't in the mood for her bubbliness, hadn't listened.

I took Olaf, knocked on Lorrie's door, said I was sorry. She didn't answer. I knocked again, went in.

She was sitting on her bed, holding Miss Pretty, her sock monkey.

I put Olaf next to them. "We could make him something. A sled?"

"I don't want him."

I said she'd feel differently in a day or so.

"I won't."

Arguing. You can guess how I feel about that. Or, I might argue myself, she was stating a fact. I couldn't figure out what to do next, was leaving when Lorrie, busying herself with Miss Pretty's red yarn braids, asked how I'd learned what happened. "Since you didn't believe me."

I apologized again, said I'd emailed her teacher so we could make things right.

"You told her I stole."

I thought she'd cry then, but she gave me a look of dry-eyed reproach, threw herself face down on the bed, moved her hand to find Olaf, sent him flying into her bookcase.

A tantrum, no excuse for that, she can cool in the same skin she got hot in, etc., but I sat down beside her, stroked her dun-colored baby hair. "Soft as a bunny's."

Another mistake. Lorrie hates her hair, wants the long, thick kind other girls have. Because she's so thin, Lisa says. It'll come, she tells Lorrie. I think Lorrie is too young to care about her appearance but Lisa has a drawer full of ribbons and bows she uses to fix Lorrie's hair.

I should have remembered the spelling bee when I saw her dress, a pretty blue plaid my mother had made her for Christmas last year, not meant for school.

Lorrie lifted her head, studied me. Her sharp little face was red, comical, and the solemn way she said she forgave me was funny too, but I thanked her, didn't laugh.

We went downstairs so I could make supper, scrambled eggs, cinnamon toast, Lorrie's favorites. Early, because she'd been too nervous about the Bee for lunch.

I bit back what I wanted to say about how she had no business missing meals.

"Shall I make cocoa?"

When Lisa came home I fixed her eggs too. Lorrie and I sat with her in the kitchen while she ate. She watched me peel an orange, taking care to remove the pith before giving it to Lorrie.

"I was mean to Lorrie this afternoon."

"A misunderstanding," Lorrie said quickly.

She wanted to talk about the spelling bee. She'd been scared, she said, standing in front of everybody. But Yessenia, her BFF since Mr. Rubio's room, now in High Achievers too, had been there and that helped. After everyone else had been eliminated, she and Yessenia went another six rounds, just the two of them. Lorrie had been afraid she'd get simultaneous, because she kept forgetting the "e", which you need for the long "a" in front of it, was relieved when Yessenia got it and spelled it right. Then Lorrie spelled nocturnal, Yessenia spelled integral, Lorrie spelled ptomaine. Yessenia missed exculpatory. Lorrie got it and the next word, sanguine, so she won.

At bedtime she told Lisa what happened. I heard her crying.

"I shouldn't have been so quick to think badly of Lorrie," I told Lisa when she came downstairs. "I've never known her to steal before."

"She didn't steal."

"I know that now."

Lisa said Lorrie is afraid of me.

She's got no reason to be, I said. "I've never hit her."

I wished I'd told her how ashamed I was.

Lisa said she was tired, went to bed. I went up too. Even when she was angry with me, slept at the edge of the mattress to avoid my touch as she did tonight, I wanted to be with her.

In the morning I could hear them in the bathroom, laughing. When they came downstairs Lorrie was wearing purple plastic grape barrettes that matched her purple T-shirt.

Cute, I remembered to say, before apologizing again.

"Are you going to keep telling her till you feel good about yourself?" Lisa asked.

We don't fight in front of Lorrie, not usually. She looked embarrassed.

At work, after the morning session got rolling, I went to offender records in the administration building. A windowless room in the basement, feels more like prison than prison.

I should have left when I saw Wojcik's high school diploma. From Chicago, some place called the Latin School. It's Kevin's job to check for GED certificates and diplomas but I might have guessed. Wojcik acts as if he's as good as anyone, better, doesn't try to make you laugh, the way Lamar does.

I had what I came for, didn't need to read what Wojcik said about not bringing a weapon because he only intended to scare her. The woman. Celeste Maundy.

She'd been contrite when she opened the door, saw him there. Like a little girl going to fetch a switch before she was sent, the way Wojcik told it, but then she'd talked back and he hit her harder than he'd meant to.

The curtains were closed when her roommate found the body. I figured Wojcik had his own key, had let himself in. I wondered if Celeste had been dreaming before she woke in the dimly lit room, saw him standing over her.

Per the police report she was Black, as Wojcik had said, but you couldn't tell from the picture. Not enough light to give a sense of color.

In the crime scene photo she's face down, legs splayed out on the shag carpet. She'd been dead for an hour then, maybe longer, but the blood seemed frank, as if still flowing. Her body had begun to swell, because of the beating. Fluids are released into the tissues in response to the trauma. Her bottom in the sweat pants was a little raised, like a sleeping baby's.

I didn't think she'd want anyone seeing her like that.

The records clerk was looking at her computer screen when I took the staples out, one by one, bending back the little metal bits, placed the picture between pieces of copy paper, put it through the shredder, took the photo bits from the trash, flushed them down the toilet in the staff bathroom, flushed again to make sure it wasn't clogged.

Wojcik had been big at birth, ten pounds, six ounces, I saw, when I made a copy of his birth certificate, stapled it where the photograph had been. It didn't belong there but if you've been in as much trouble as Wojcik has, your records are big and unwieldy and things get misplaced.

In the shift office I infracted Wojcik for lying and failure to program.

He was unassigned from school, would have to take the first job available. In the kitchen, in the dish pit, where the temperature, even on the coldest day of winter, doesn't get below 85 degrees. He'd start at 5:00 am, return to his unit at 3:30 pm for count. He won't have much time for the Dirty White Boys now, Captain Reese said, pleased.

What I thought was getting rid of Wojcik meant another inmate would get a shot at compromising Ms. Goodwin.

When I came to take Wojcik from her class she stood, as if to follow.

I took my time marching him past the other classrooms, wanting the other offenders to see.

"I'd really like to say goodbye to Monica."

"You may send Ms. Goodwin a kite." Kites are the little yellow forms offenders use to communicate with prison employees. The mailroom staff read them before they're delivered.

"I just need a few minutes. But I guess you can't help."

A popular technique with offenders, implying you're too low on the food chain to have any power, makes you want to prove them wrong.

"You're right!"

I was with my crew at the officer's station, when Ms. Goodwin came.

"A word, Sergeant."

I saw my officers exchanging looks. They'd think I was weak, letting her to talk to me like that.

"Certainly, Ms. Goodwin."

I had her sit with her back to the window in my office, so no one could see her crying. "You don't think about how much he has to give. All you care about is the rulebook."

"You knew he had a diploma?"

"Of course I knew. He graduated with honors."

She could be fired for participating in Wojcik's deception.

"So you lied."

She squirmed, said no one had asked her.

"You also have something to offer, Ms. Goodwin. The offenders often tell me how much they enjoy your class."

She shows movies on Fridays.

"I don't see it as just a job. Everyone has given up on them. Everyone except me."

Christ.

Be careful, I said. "If he sends you a kite you can answer. Say you wish him well in the future, whatever. But don't try to get in touch with him yourself and, if he contacts you at home, report him."

I reminded her of the mental health counselor who'd been fired last year, charged with First Degree Custodial Sexual Misconduct.

She bridled. It's so hard here, she said, everyone suspecting you.

She didn't deserve the chance I'd given her, would likely waste it.

"We need you, Ms. Goodwin."

Kevin came by at quitting time to congratulate me on Lorrie's win. "Though Cody gave her a run for her money."

I remembered Cody from the potluck. A big kid, sullen. After he'd cleaned his plate he said he wanted to be with his friends. I watched him load another plate with food, take it, and a bag of Fritos, under the bleachers, where he ate alone.

"Roger that."

Lorrie must have been smarting from yesterday, because she was waiting on the school steps, ran to the car as soon as she saw me.

On the way home she said she'd wanted to give Olaf to Yessenia.

You should have asked Mommy or me for permission, I didn't say.

But she and Yessenia decided to give it to Mr. Rubio instead. "The little ones like to hold lovies during story time."

She sounded so important, I wanted to ask when the school would make her principal.

"That was a nice thing for you girls to do." I said. Holding back didn't come easily. "Do you miss being in Mr. Rubio's room?"

Yes. Every morning, when she went in the school she wanted to turn right for his room, instead of going upstairs to High Achievers, where they called her a freak and a baby and nobody liked her except Yessenia. "I hate it there."

Don't ask if you don't want to know. I wanted to tell her how stupid she was for still wanting to pretend to warm a toy bottle in a tiny saucepan on a toy stove.

When Mrs. Swenson gave them their work back, she would tell the class how well Lorrie had done, better than anybody. This embarrassed Lorrie but she was afraid to say anything, finally got up the nerve. "She wasn't mad. She said 'I'll just write nice things on your papers instead, because you always get me thinking, girlfriend.'"

I wondered if Cody was one of the ones giving Lorrie a hard time.

Today Tsumugi, her Japanese tutor, had shown her how to fold paper to make one of those garrison caps stewardesses used to wear, let her make an extra one for Yessenia. Lorrie was the flight attendant and Tsumugi was the passenger, a demanding one, asking for food, drinks, magazines. "We have so much fun. Sometimes I pretend to myself she's my big sister. Do you think that's silly?"

"No."

She looked relieved, said she loved math too. Science was great. They had their own computers. The field trip to see the hawks was interesting and she had second lunch now so that was good and there was another girl she liked, too, Charlotte, and somebody named Andrew was nice, telling her about books he thought she'd like.

So if everything's more or less all right why did she have to jerk me around like that?

At home I had her put her cap on, took a picture of her looking proud and excited. Like a brand new airline employee, I told her.

"It's just pretend," she said. "I'm not pretty enough to be a flight attendant."

A few minutes before she'd been laughing about how much easier it was to give the safety announcement in English than Japanese.

I could tell her that looks don't matter. It's what's on the inside that counts. Why would you want to be a flight attendant anyway?

But that was of no use to her, I knew, and I was glad when she let me lift her into my arms, hold her against my chest, tell her I thought she was pretty. "Pretty as a rose, pretty as Reese's Cups. Pretty as a one-hundred-dollar bill. Just extremely pretty."

I knew she wasn't convinced but she smiled. "Daddy, do you even know who is on a one-hundred-dollar bill?" She sounding cagey, had something up her sleeve.

"Indeed I do, Miss Smart. Benjamin Franklin."

"And which president was he?" Still cagey.

I tossed her up, loving her thin excited shriek, loved her boldness, caught her. "If you're going to mess with me, Missy, I'll mess with you. Everyone knows Benjamin Franklin was too busy inventing Pokemon to be president."

Stiff as a board, I must have sounded to her. I've never been good at having fun with Lorrie, but I was doing it.

I threw her again. When she fell back in my arms I held on to her giggling young self.

"Oh, Daddy."

Oh Lorrie.

- Jane Snyder

The Jesus Bed

You are not like us; this bed has history,

> peasant grief hammered into heavy round balls
> of teakwood from trees on a hot Bali night.

Those strangers never spoke our names

> or drank dopamine on the sea of sweat,
> crashing on the rocks of a thousand lost nights,

but others certainly did.

> The tempted & tangled pretty boy gods whose
> pipe smoke, no hope, apparitions of lust

made chat lines buzz with promise & ruin,

> as the body turned ghost before love had a chance to
> sleep in the Jesus bed.

- Daniel Moore

In Love

I will leave you after you are saved in love,
return to the dams that were caved in love.

Let me nurse the pain, flood the ache, pour it like wine into rain.
No — free me, but only a little. I want to hurt, be enslaved in love.

The battle is lost, what do I do with the enemy's map?
Every rose, ocean, blade you gave I braved in love.

Krishna, a sapphire of infinity, loves all men's wives — who can
blame beauty for desiring mirrors? Even God is depraved in love.

Have you ever loved anyone enough to leave yourself?
I sang, awoke, wept, cleaned — hell, even shaved in love.

Thunder has lost its light, lightning its passion to punish.
No bones remain to be rattled in graves once paved in love.

Kisses begin in tongue, end in teeth — you confuse mercy
with revenge. Even your curses, Shannan, are engraved in love.

- Shannan Mann

For God

Mobilize soldiers, tonight we will hunt for God.
Peel the skin off the skeletons that burnt for God.

Your green hair raped, blue blood drained. But Earth, eat
your rage. Could man consume anything if it weren't for God?

The moment their meat is teethed from bones,
who do the calves and babes grunt for? God!

At ease, battalion, drink, lick sugar, lay with your love. We need
not ravage like Him, the blade of devotion is too blunt for God.

When He comes, do not let Him speak —
words, weather, sex — all mere stunts for God.

The trap He set for me has caught His leg instead, now
He sobs in my arms: Shannan, even God hunts for God.

- Shannan Mann

Family

Here, read my palm, make a language of touch, make a family.
Why do you go away, make me watch as you break a family?

Agni and Soma light white the night. Who
knew even the sun and sea can bake a family?

Who's eating who? Feel no fear to gut the duck
who plucks a fish who bites a snake: ah family!

Mama's left and papa's always right
in rehearsing how to forsake a family.

The neighbours are looking, come on, hold each
other's hands, don't forget how to fake a family.

We were glass wind and water. Who
raised us to be so opaque? Our family.

Childless, Adam and Eve would have remained naked.
Cain and Abel happened because of a snake — a family.

So much has the power to kill us — a flood, space
debris, a dream, icicles, an earthquake, our family.

Begin in becoming and end after coming — so fickle
a flicker of flesh a flume a fuck a fleck a flake a family.

For years you've crawled on the bed of the ocean, break
the surface, Shannan, I swear no more will it ache — a family.

- Shannan Mann

Found

A harbour I looked for, an abyss I found.
Love — an echo, a naked wound, a cold sound.

The melody is gone, the chorus is a single voice,
the violins gather dust, the psalms all drowned.

Save the world and feed yourself with its famine.
The gravedigger's grave is not dug in the ground.

Vengeance belongs to the Lord, victory to me. I let
no one look (unlike Him) at the thorns in my crown.

If I live I will need to mother my bruises. If I smile —
repay another's debt. Even in freedom, bound.

Return me my rainstorm, give me back my rags. I confess
nothing. Not to a priest, a lover, hell or the hellhound.

- Shannan Mann

The Pain

At a time like this you should relieve the pain.
Why — when it goes — do you grieve the pain?

A rain of dust, a dry river, this lonely country
stands by a window again to receive the pain.

Trust yourself if you cannot trust another
scheme. Worship faults, believe the pain.

Even love is one letter away from hiding its hand.
How many kisses will it take to deceive the pain?

When your childhood monsters creep up
weep them a lullaby so they can perceive the pain.

In a silent, abandoned garden I grow life to elixir
my body, my baby dying on Christmas eve, the pain.

Shannan, you have written it all down now, hoping
people in pages can feel — how naive! — the pain.

- Shannan Mann

Old Stones

" 'Not all our power is gone—not all our fame—
'Not all the magic of our high renown—' "

--- From Edgar Allan Poe, *The Coliseum*

The tourist wandered, seeking solace in the pale stones, a sign from the rock-rose and the saxifrage, some augury from headless gods, their arms uplifted, gleanings from a fractured frieze, an earnest from antiquity. That evening, a pebble from the site, lodged in a wandering shoe, whispered faint sentences in an ancient tongue, a syllogism or a prayer, as the tourist sought the source of the wonder, an incantation or a warning, as the tourist looked in vain for the voice. Later that night, all babies born developed powers of flight, the nearest rivers reversed their flow, the Internet woke briefly (to its own future, as demonstrated by the past), a man named by no one became a judge, and so to the end. The next morning, the tourist found a stone in the soles of a shoe, a keep-sake, a fragment of architrave, a shard from a column. She forgot the stone during the day's Internet outages and the rumors of rivers returning to their sources. But the stone smiled, and the ruins did the same.

- Daniel Rabuzzi

Carry Me

"You tell if that dog's tied?" Wade had his face up to the windshield.

The dog in question was an old black lab with a grizzled muzzle. It was flopped on its side in the yard's long grass, and I wasn't entirely sure it wasn't dead.

"I don't think he's dangerous."

"I was bit as a boy," Wade said. He pulled up the left leg of his pants to show me four puncture wounds, so old now they looked like dimples.

"Like I said, I think you're safe."

Wade and I had been working together for about a month. He did not strike me as a very bright individual, and I was put off by his swept-back, duck-tailed hair style, but he was surprising in ways that made me appreciate him as a partner. Nearly every day he would say or do something that I had not anticipated, and I appreciated the diversions. Once he told me he had spent a short period of time in prison. He never told me how long exactly or what he had done to be put away, but I was not all that concerned. I had seen enough of him to dispel any fear that he might be a killer or capable of other acts of violence. In my mind, he had unsuccessfully robbed a convenience store. I think more than anything it was his straightforward nature that distinguished him. Nothing was anything but what it seemed to be. I suppose that kind of outlook made life a less complicated proposition.

I picked up the invoice from the seat between Wade and me and checked the address, which I knew was correct, but I needed to be sure because, even though we're not angels of death, we are the ones who bring the bad news, the ones who announce what's inevitable. Showing up at the wrong house might be a shock to those whose door we wrongly knocked on, and our delay in getting to the right place would cause undue and unwanted distress to people already suffering.

We got out of the van and started toward the house, Wade slipping to the side of me farthest from the dog. He watched it warily the whole way to the porch steps, but the poor old animal did not so much as open an eye. I couldn't help but notice as we walked that, even though the house was like all of the rest of the comfortable houses on this comfortable street, there was an air of neglect about the place. The lawn was overgrown, newspapers—soggy despite being bagged in plastic—lay on the driveway, maybe a week's worth, and mail poked from the box mounted by the front door. More than that, though, everything seemed sad, as if what was going on inside cast a spell that somehow muffled sound and stilled the air. I had experienced this kind of thing before, but I wondered if Wade felt it, too.

"This seem odd to you in any way?" I asked.

"You mean the dog?"

"No. The whole place. Kind of a weird vibe."

"Somebody's dying. That's why, I'd guess."

When we got to the bottom of the steps up to the porch that stretched across the front of the house, a woman came out and waited until we got to the top. She had her arms wrapped around herself in a kind of self-protective hug I had seen many times before. Her hair was pulled back poorly, and her clothes were rumpled: both familiar signs of heartache and worry. She tried to smile, but it didn't last long. She held the door open and didn't look at us when we moved past into the house.

"The room is this way." She pointed toward a hallway that ran straight to the back of the house, past an open stairway. We started after her in that direction.

"My husband isn't here," she said. "He travels for work. But we talked before he left."

When we went past an open door, I looked in and saw a young woman under blankets in a leather recliner, her head wrapped in a red turban. She looked at me, and I looked away, reminded too much of my sister in a similar pose. I followed the woman—the mother—the rest of the way down the hall to a room that had recently been cleared of furniture. The walls were a pale yellow, and the smell of paint was in the air. My best guess was that it had been an office or a den, not an essential living space, which was usually the case when we came to a house to set up the bed and do whatever else the family wanted. Most of what we did and saw on these visits was the same.

After my sister died, my brother-in-law Brad started Hope and Glory Hospice Services. Pam and I had been close since we were kids, and it was hard for both Brad and me to watch her waste away. He had it worse, of course, because she wanted to be at home and he was with her the whole time. I visited when I could, when I was sober enough not to start crying and making a scene. Not long after the funeral, Brad told me his plan to start a company that would provide the kind of care he and Pam never got. Then he told me he wanted me to work for him. At the time, I was changing oil in cars, a mindless job that suited me then. The catch, he explained, was that I had to give up drinking. Six years later, I'm still on the job.

The mother, who had not identified herself but whose last name I knew from the invoice was Stafford, gestured toward the only window in the room.

"I think Sam would like the bed there, where there's some light from outside." She looked at me for confirmation. I took a look out the window and saw a fenced back yard with unattended flower beds and a big oak tree that shaded about half the space.

"That's what we'll do," I said. I turned to say something to Wade—not anything important, just something to give him a chance to speak to the mother and get used to it—but he wasn't there. I turned a bit more and saw him standing in the doorway of the room where I'd seen the young woman. Then he stepped into the room and out of sight.

"I'll just get my partner," I said. I left her standing in the room and went back down the hallway, stopping at the door Wade had gone through. He was kneeling next to the chair and the young woman was leaning forward, talking to him. I couldn't hear anything, but Wade clearly could. He nodded his head slowly. When the young woman saw me, she apparently told Wade I was there. He got up quickly, then reached out his hand and lay it for a moment on her shoulder before coming with me out to the van.

I yanked open the back doors of the van so that Wade would know I was angry with him. Before I could chew him out, he apologized.

"I know I wasn't supposed to do that," he said. He slid the ramp out and set it down so we could wheel the bed out. "She smiled, so I went in. Her name's Samantha."

"Wade, do you know why you're not supposed to talk with the patients?" I walked up the ramp to where the folded-up bed was and started to undo the straps that held it in place.

"Because it reminds them of how sick they are."

"More or less."

"But she already knows. She said she's been sick most of her life."

I got behind the bed and moved it forward, toward the ramp. Wade guided it from the front.

"How can that be that she's been sick her whole life and never had a chance to be happy? How does that happen"

"I don't know, Wade. It's what happens sometimes."

"She said she doesn't want to die here in this house. She wants to go to some lovely place she's never been. That was her word: lovely."

I pushed the bed to the front steps, and the two of us lifted it up to the porch.

"She told you quite a lot," I said. "What got her started? You say something?"

"I didn't say anything. She just started talking."

Before I could scold him more, a white SUV with the Hope and Glory logo on the door pulled into the driveway next to the van. We stopped to wait until Dorothy got out and joined us. She usually arrived at the same time as we did because it was her job to talk with the family before we moved things inside, but when Wade and I left for here she said she would be a little late due to an issue with insurance at another home. Apparently, there were many such issues, and I was glad my job did not require me dealing with that sort of thing.

Dorothy was a strongly built woman and used her size to her advantage. When she first started at Hope and Glory, I took offense at her high-handed manner, and she made it clear she did not appreciate my sour moods. We got so we could work together and not give the other too much trouble, though there were times when I could be irritated by her ways, and I suspect the same was true for her when it came to me. Wade had not been around long enough to stand up to her yet, so when she got to where we were waiting on the porch, he stepped back behind me, the way he had with the dog, and kept his eyes down. Dorothy opened the black folder she always carried and held out her hand. I took the invoice from my shirt pocket and handed it to her.

"What can you tell me?" she said.

"The bed's going in a room at the back of the house. It's empty, so no problem there."

"How are the parents?"

"It's just the mom. Dad's on a business trip."

"Of course he is," Dorothy said. She closed her folder and went inside.

"She could've held the door for us," Wade said.

"Yes," I said," she could've." I let it drop there.

We wheeled the bed into the house and down the hallway to the room where it would be set up. Wade looked in at the young woman when we passed the door, but I kept focused ahead. Dorothy and the mother were in the room, and Dorothy indicated a spot next to the window where we were to put the bed. Then they left us to it. When we had it in place, unfolded with the wheels locked and the bed rails attached, I put on the fitted sheet, smoothing it to make sure there were no creases that could cause bedsores. Wade had gone to the window and opened it to let in some fresh air.

"I can't stand that paint smell," he said. "Gives me a headache."

Dorothy called to us from the room where the young woman was. I let Wade lead the way.

The mother was standing next to the recliner and Dorothy stood next to her, an arm draped around the woman's shoulders. A wheelchair had been pushed close to the recliner, which meant it was time to move the young woman to the bed. Normally, that meant getting the patient into the chair, moving all of the blankets and pillows and other things they kept with them for comfort, and then getting the person situated in the bed we brought. When the

107

mother loosened the blankets, I could see how fragile the young woman was, like a bird, like my sister had looked. She lay her head back, then reached up and pushed the red turban back off her forehead. Wade and I got into position on either side of the recliner and made ready.

"No," she said. "I don't want the chair." She looked at Wade and held out her arms. "Carry me."

For a moment, no one did anything. Dorothy, I suspected, was trying to figure out a kind way to say no. The mother looked from her daughter to Wade to Dorothy to me. Wade just looked at the young woman and then leaned down and lifted her up, cradling her. She rested her head against his shoulder and wrapped her arms around her neck. Wade closed his eyes and appeared to take a deep breath. I gathered up the bedding and went on ahead. I put the pillows at the head of the bed but waited with the blankets. Wade came into the room followed by the mother and Dorothy. He bent forward and laid the young woman on the mattress, staying put until she let go of him. I arranged the blankets over her as best I could. I knew it would all be re-arranged after we left.

Dorothy and the mother and I went to the kitchen to go over details, but Wade stayed there with the young woman. After all of the paperwork was signed and visits arranged and Dorothy left, it became uncomfortable for both the mother and me to keep up any kind of conversation, so I went to the room and told Wade we had to leave. I waited another ten minutes in the truck before he showed up. He got in and didn't say a word for most of the ride. Finally, a few blocks from Hope and Glory, he turned to me and said he was going back to get the young woman.

"Not right now," he said. "But some night soon. I left the back window unlocked and told her I'd be coming."

"That's not a good idea, Wade, for a lot of reasons."

"Maybe not."

"There's the mother for one thing."

"She sleeps upstairs. They have one of those baby monitors."

"OK. Beyond that, what's your plan?"

"I don't really have one yet, but I'm going to take her some lovely place that she's never seen. I just need to figure things out."

I can't say why that girl put such faith in Wade. I don't know what she saw in him that made her feel he would be her champion, but that was what apparently happened, and Wade was only too glad to oblige.

"Don't tell me anything else," I said. "When you get caught, I don't want to be considered an accomplice."

"I won't get caught," Wade said. "What I'm going to do is the right thing. You can't get caught if you do the right thing."

"Don't be so sure."

We left the truck in the parking lot and went inside to see if there was anything else to do. It was less than fifteen minutes until quitting time, so Brad told us to go on home. Tomorrow would be a busier day he said, and we would probably end up working late. He did not mention anything about Wade's improper behavior, which meant Dorothy had decided to let it slide. She was at her desk on the phone when we walked out, and I was glad again that I did not have her job. Wade said he would see me in the morning and then got into his sagging wreck of a car and drove away in a cloud of blue exhaust. I got into my own car and sat there a minute before starting the engine. I could see into Brad's office and watched him at his desk, looking at his computer screen and rubbing his cheek.

I know I owe Brad a lot. He gave me a good job and a good life. He was a great husband to Pam, and I can't thank him enough for that. Almost two years ago, he got married again. His new wife was divorced and had two boys. Brad and Pam didn't have enough time together to start a family, but they had both wanted children someday. I'm happy for Brad, but I also feel a little lost. When Pam was alive, especially when she was getting sicker by the day, Brad and I became friends. We took care of each other just as much as we tried to take care of her. After she died and I went to work for him, Brad and I went out for dinner every few weeks. We still had Pam then, memories of her, and that was enough to keep us in pretty close contact for almost four years. After he met his new wife and had a new family, that changed. He didn't need Pam any more. Not that he ever forgot her, but now he had someone else to think about, someone else to share things with.

I did not. Pam was my little sister and her dying hurt me every day. I had no one and nothing to take her place. That's why I could not look at the young woman today. She reminded me too much of Pam the day she died: waxy, pale skin, sad eyes that seemed too large for her face, hands that floated weakly when she moved them. It was just the two of us in their living room. She was curled up on the couch under an ugly brown and gold afghan our mother had made. A nurse had just left after giving her something for the pain, and I told Brad to go out for a walk. He hadn't left Pam's side for hours. I pulled the afghan up and tucked it around her and she died. I could hear her sigh and saw in her eyes that she was gone. It was so quick. Whenever I was sent to a house where a young woman was dying, I remembered that day. It's why the air would seem so still and sound would be muffled. It happened every time.

Brad looked out the window and saw me. He waved and I waved, then

I drove home. On the way, I thought about Wade and what he was thinking of doing. He stayed with me all through dinner and even when I'd finished watching television and had gotten into bed. I had a hard time imagining Wade would go through with it, but maybe. Maybe he would drive his crappy car to that neighborhood and park it a few blocks away because of its not having a decent muffler. Maybe he would sneak around the back of the house and let himself in through the window. Maybe he would lift the girl from her bed, and she would put her arms around his neck like she had before. Maybe he would walk through the house, out the front door, past the decrepit dog still lying on the lawn, out into the night. Maybe he would put her in the passenger seat, get behind the wheel, look over at her and say, "I know just the place."
And maybe he would be right.

- Patrick Parks

110

Winner *Julia Darling Memorial Poetry Prize*
Somewhere in America

I knew where I was, though I couldn't have named
the place. Raspberries held the woods back
with green razor wire. Grass gone to seed
rubbed against the silvered out-buildings: sheds,
granary, an old milk house. I stood at each,
laid a hand against their cool, cupped boards
as if saying goodbye. Inside would be all the cars
I ever owned: the tan Rambler, the German Opel,
my grandpa's black Ford Galaxy.
                                            I walked
until I came into the town. Late sun filtered
through elm leaves, the twilight air soft
to the touch. Returning from work, men
stopped with one foot up on curb or step,
stretched a little, unhurried, minds on
their own business. I wanted to approach them,
to say I too love my socket set and claw hammer,
the sad song of beer and baseball.
I too own a box of blurry snapshots
and call it home.
                        The men murmured
to each other or into their hands, lingering
near their pickup trucks, where sulky Calvins
pissed on tailgates. I read, or thought I read,
something in their eyes and looked away,
kept on walking, too frozen up inside
to speak the simple fact—"Brother!"

Scott Lowery

The Story Itself

Bean had a mole below his left eye. The kids in our 5th class teased him, said he had chocolate on his face. I was the one who knew it was his left eye, not the right. Who listened in secret to songs like Baby Love by the Supremes.

Bean didn't carry pocket knives to school, or look up girls' skirts. Nor would he steal the juice box off your desk when you weren't looking.

He had immaculate Ticonderoga erasers, made my knee socks droop, my weak bony ankles, weaker. At recess, a soft piece of tar was thrown at my feet. I looked up and there he was, skipping backward, wanting me to chase him.

So much depended upon the chalk drawings on the school pavement, on the creamy yellows and waxy pinks, on hopping between the lines.

As Bean watched, he pulled on his mole, mulishly. His skin got stretchy as an old nylon stocking. His patchy clothes could've belonged to a paid mourner.

When we went in, Mrs. Rivers hugged him. The boys guffawed, their laughter, croaking, like old cars, the kind everyone junked in their front yards, old, rusty, sunk in maudlin mud.

Ours was a misfit purity. In art, we swapped scissors, blades aimed forward. We looked as if we'd done something dangerous.

The scissor handles were inked in handwriting not our own. They were marked by our mothers, carefully, the way they marked us as we made our way into the world.

Time may disfigure us all, just not Bean, nor those scissors which I still have, like a tinny kind of history.

Nothing touches Bean. Not the cruelty of children, nor the gravel that pushed its way into his restless body. Not the ugliness of Edgar's hearse which came too late, nor the small grass square that mothers him.

At the funeral parlor, I got no further than taking a holy card; a picture of an angel as dark-haired as him, an angel I shred into ribbons in the parking lot, in my plaid skirt, which is where Edgar found me, took my hand, said, "Tis a pity, Pit."

In the ensuing silence, its odorlessness, Edgar, a grown man, withdrew his hands, half-hid them in his shirtsleeves. He then got back into his hearse, which looked like doubt, or a shot body. As he drove away, his ears flapped, an elephant's.

Standing there, I remembered how Bean traced my 5th grade body with poster paint, legs V-shaped, like the outline of a victim at a crime scene.

I was the only girl partnered with a boy—his nails filthy from prying back the onion grass, bug shells crunched up in his teeth because he liked the sound.

Bean refused all paint colors except blue. Leaning over me, his lips heavy with focus, I watched his tongue as he dragged the paintbrush, like a lit match in a room full of gasoline.

The girls called it brave, letting him trace me, or so they said as we got in line to leave the classroom.

When I got home, my mother hung the poster, full length on the fridge. The white space something I stepped from, the blue line still wobbly between my thighs where his hands shook.

It held the work and charm of memory. Two whole notes at rest as the outline darkened in.

My mother went to her room, blitzed her hair with Aqua Net after drawing electric blue lines under her eyes. As I stared at her through an empty paper towel tube, like a spyglass, I thought about the translucence of the eternal.

This as a ball slapped down the flower-bothered court across the street. It had a rhythm, like saying the rosary, or brushing teeth. I won't describe it, nor do I want to describe how Bean stood before that train with the alertness of a small god.

All anyone should know is that I felt cold, helpless. Even the sun caught on, growing red-rimmed around the eyes. Every wound deserves a close-up, just not Bean's. I'll never understand how he felt, which is why I'm still covered in shame.

Shame because I couldn't shove him off the tracks, the weight of him immense. It sorrowed me how he still smelled of the paint that sloughed our poster.

This as the train screeched on and on, like hot, pink monkeys. No one told me how alone I'd be, no one.

At school, Bean and I often bumped elbows, like a secret code, or the tight geometry of kites. Which is why the boys taunted us. "Beanie-weenie," they yelled, "we want you to race Pit the dimwit."

If I lost, the boys promised to take me into the woods where they'd yank down my panties among the fretted leaves. The boy who would become my husband, Lou, was among them. He even whistled, a thin sound, like a needle in a vein.

There was no way I was going to let Bean beat me, no way some boys would yank off my panties. This as they chalked a line on the sidewalk, wavy as an angel, bluish, shallow, vague.

Bean and I toed the line. He smelled like ironed mittens as I pulled up my knee socks, snapped the rubber band, for luck.

When they yelled, Go, I tore down the sidewalk. The cement looked like itty, bitty mountains. I ran as hard as I could. My lungs beat, like bats with frozen wings. I ran as if the sidewalk were a runway, but to where?

A sterilized heaven full of the dejected, the abysmal, the utterly deplored, who were the only ones I could fathom, let alone love.

Even my breath was ice-picked. As was Bean's. When I heard him huff, I ran harder. His limbs had a doll-like swish.

I thought about the unbearable, light as batting, but bloodless. The moment considered me, as I considered it. The boys, they heckled. My insides felt like mayonnaise, or sour milkweed, but I had blood, gourds of it, gross, glorious.

The sidewalk was a long slow slide. When the boys yelled, "I want to eat your panty face," I ran harder, faster, couldn't stop.

Not even for Bean. Whom I loved. Not even for him, or his chocolate mole, even though he loved blue, the way I loved yellow.

Bean whose lips were rubbery, like a flyswatter. Who would not win. No then, not ever. His breath felted me. It was patchwork breath that'd been worked over, like the tiniest breath of the tiniest baby.

The boys kept baiting us. "Beanie-weenie. Pit, you dimwit, whore us." They were ghastly pale as I ran too hard, too fast, until my body simply gave out, a bassinet flipped onto the ground.

My knee was stripped. The flesh, a scalped goose, fell away like feathers, a catastrophe of feathers, briny as pickle juice. What fell out of me—loose baggies of blood—bobbled on my knee socks, gangly as nerves.

I sucked my knee as though its baldness implicated me in something as strict and tantalizing as evil. The blood tasted like Bean's. Salt that's been grated, seized, rubbed into a wound that signaled the bitterest of defeats.

When Bean knelt beside me, I bit him. My teethmarks railroaded his hand, which flapped, a sick fish. I bit him again, hummed, Baby Love.

The boys just stood there, exact witnesses whose exact work was to watch me. As soon as they hunkered around me, Bean took off.

This was their work. To drag me into the woods. Eat my panties. As though a fifth grader's icky, old underwear could deliver them.

Into what? Nothing musical, nothing kind, but furious. Like a girl, or a Mom.

Days later, when I found those panties inside my desk with the crotch cut out, I felt godless, possessed, shamed. Had Lou stuffed them in there, like a reckless exhibition?

In that classroom, we were all persecuted, especially Bean, who accepted Mrs. River's hug without a word. His silence made him cuter, sweeter, like Rainbow Sparkle Pony, who I hid in my backpack. Hadn't my father stuck decals of naked ladies all over her as a joke?

Hadn't I then stuck those decals all over Bean's dog, Tiny, who looked clownish, especially as she tried to bite them off, like a harassment of flies?

I thought about those decals as Bean stood in front of the class, still as a praying mantis. I went up to him, took his hand, which felt scurrilous, as if it had been stuffed into a waffle iron.

I kissed him, my lips all pursy, squishy even. The sound they made was like the zipper on my pencil pouch, the one embossed with a Smiley face.

Everyone applauded, but the applause was more like spit, wads and scads of it, shooting across the classroom, greenish, ghoulish.

Arcs of it like a storyline, but whatever the story was, I wanted to abolish it. I curtsied, walked right out of the classroom, escorting Bean as if to chauffeur him into a world where his mother, Lenore, might drive by.

She didn't. By then, she'd wandered off, dreaming about babies—clay babies, cake babies, pineal babies, or ones that looked like pink flamingoes.

She dreamt only about these babies—long babies, short babies, babies that sounded like gills, babies who were never scolded, or strangled, or set on fire.

As I helped Bean home, he tore out his hair, like pages from a girly magazine, then stared at his mother's sewing machine, which looked like a petite dinosaur.

The stillness of the thing. That's what was the matter. Patches all over the house, the after-color of whales.

Lenore was gone. As were her babies. Whom she told no one about, especially not Bean. Only her apron remained, hung on its hook, thin as a twig.

Bean looked like an empty candy wrapper as he listened to the rain speaking in a language the sheltered never understand.

We listened to the owlets, the wind tossing the cottonwood leaves, the little foxes dropping little mouthfuls of lilies from their teeth to bark at the mountains behind the barn.

Ontario, Illinois was a beautiful place, but also ugly. It was a place where we crawled through the tall grass, our chests against the earth so we could hear the river underground.

It held no stories of damnation, or miracles. It was a place where we were prisms breaking light into color. It even had a graveyard.

That night as I lay awake, I knew Bean had gone off with his dog, Tiny, to look for his mom.

Was she trembling in some ditch? In the snow? Was Tiny's bark, snapping with the excitement of the hunt? By kerosene? By moonlight?

The dog's yelps, like an antidote to death, rattled in the gutters of Bean's chest. There was cause for concern, for caution, but the ground was pure as the denouncement of a mirror. And he was nowhere to be seen.

We knew each other's insides and why we cried, but what Bean did out there I'll never know, only that it's in the space between my words, which have never been the same.

When he came back, he said, "Don't look at it. Don't even try to remove it from my shoe."

I looked down, saw a scrap of Lenore's dress, wondered what it would be like to lose your mother. Did she throb inside his ears?

Asking him about her, he made a sound like loose shoelaces, or the echo of urine in a toilet.

I stayed the night to lullaby him to sleep. When I got home, my grandmother was sewing birds back into the quilt. Their wings, they whimpered, like kittens.

I sat alongside her, on that green sofa, wrapped in fabulous plastic, like vaseline. As I tried to say what happened in a breath or two, everything seemed like the remnant of something else.

I crawled into her lap, which was the mist I parted in order to become the mist, and wept. Oh how I wept in her lap, which was ample, a long green valley. There was silk in it, or animals, or lost babies and that's why I loved her.

The weeping went on, like a very long story and the thing about stories is that they don't really end, they just pretend to.

Grandma looked at me, asked, "do you remember Lizard's golden thread, how it could never end?"

"Yes, but does that have to do with Bean?"

"Didn't it weave a story like veils full of fear, thrill, ennui—golden it was, as it unspooled, like a treasure chest full of lavender horses, wheat sheafs, tall as amorous men?"

"Wasn't it made of words, no, the sky, its customary glamour, soft as prayer, which is never the answer? Doesn't that thread weave you to Bean?"

This when I told her how the train came, the one that stacked him up, like bricks, or dirty thoughts. He was covered with dirt, bolts of loose blood, as he lay on those tracks, like a wineglass stomped on at a wedding.

The crows in the branches tendered no apologies, but shrieked, as did Tiny, who was still held together by my father's decals of naked, impervious ladies.

Bean's toe poked out of his boot, like a brown offering. I looked at his shoelaces, wanted to flee because he was an abomination I couldn't yet abide.

I wasn't much more than a child, cut as we all are from living flesh, from bone, from skull. I patted Bean, like a very quiet pancake, said, "please don't do this again."

I went to the dog, who was covered by those irascible decals, dumb as dots. Which I picked off as Tiny licked me, like a postage stamp, or the way my father licked me.

The licking, the incessant licking, smeared all over me, like the guts of a fly, which my father rubbed into me, gritty, as the paintbrushes Bean and I used to slough our poster.

And the message, or the meaning, it's the dog. Of course, I took Tiny home, those decals stuffed in my pockets, like Girl Scout badges. Merit badges.

In the end, it's always the dog, compliant as a child, but for its incessant tail, like a windshield wiper, back and forth, back and forth, light as bells, bells.

- Elizabeth Kirschner

Thoughts at 2:30 a.m.

I resent the cliche of "broken"
Too clean, too neat
Where's the rot, the infection?
Where are the scars I was promised?

My heart is not pottery
Mended with gold or with glue
If only it were that fragile

Shall I show you what it is?
Take a knife, place it at my clavicle
Draw it down between my breasts, split the bone
And watch what spills out
Like the guts of an eviscerated animal

- Kaitlyn Bancroft

In Which I Loved You in the Desert

This is the definition of insanity:
You hold water to my lips, then take it away
Again and again and again
And each time, I truly believe you'll let me drink

The sun commits slow violence on my head
Did you know you can almost live on the fantasy of water?

And did you know
When I stood on our glorious red rocks and fell forward
I knew you wouldn't catch me
But still felt betrayed when the desert ground broke me?

- Kaitlyn Bancroft

Soccer

Your dentist found a cavity. You never had one as a child, you say. Why do I not know that? What mother doesn't know the story of her daughter's mouth? You were a scrappy girl, a fierce midfield defender with dark bangs beside your blond friend Grace. You handled pickups, dropoffs with aplomb—practices, lessons, games played on the too-green grass between North and South Slope, your father's neighborhood and mine. *Soccer* is British schoolboy slang for Association Football, a short form that sidesteps *ass,* though *ass* stays in the mind. Grace's mom divorced Coach Altman years ago, their place on Seventh Street a Starbucks now. You ask me, as if I might know, how little your dental will pay.

- Hilary Sideris

Coney Island Avenue

It ends where Brooklyn ends, where dropped shells shatter on black rock,
wave and gull call and respond, *Shhh* follows *What the fuck*. Remy rubs my
feet at Dolphin Spa, asks "Water good?" I nod though it's so hot it hurts.
Girls on cells talk wedding, gel, shellac. My paper casing breaks. Island Blue
smudge. There's only one man here, the manager. He wears a tight t-shirt, an
image I can't make out—mushroom cloud, jellyfish, human skull? Is that a
wig, hat, yarmulka, his head? I tell him it's my fault, not hers, but he insists
she touch me up. I tuck ten dollars in the envelope that bears her name, not in
her hand. Twisted tissue between my toes, I flipflop to the Q, ascend the steps
to a platform where cannibal pigeons peck a hot wing.

- Hilary Sideris

Mannheim Train Station at Midnight

I was only there to change trains:
my train from Vienna arrived at ten p.m.,
my train to Berlin left at seven in the morning.
I looked for a quiet spot on the plastic chairs
and took out my Neruda, *Veinte poemas de amor
y una canción desesperada.* I picked it up
in Madrid, needed to work on my Spanish. I
had all night. I could recognize half of the nouns,
but my tenses were wrong and I didn't have a dictionary.
I tried reading out loud, listening to the rhythms
and sounds instead of comprehending the words.

I wasn't sure if the train station would stay open
all night. The last trains had arrived and departed.
I didn't speak German and the information desk
had closed for the day. I traveled by whim,
going from city to city when I felt ready,
no guidebooks, no maps, just a faith
in the EurRail system and a month pass.

The molded chairs were not designed for sleep,
each one separate. A station employee
in a jumpsuit asked me to join him for a drink,
said he needed to work on his English.
He called me golden boy and invited me
to his apartment for the night.
His English was better than my Spanish.
Instead I spent the night with Neruda
and a tongue I couldn't master.

- Michael Hardin

Swim Meet

My son is fourteen,
freshman at his first
meet after two years

lost to the pandemic—
the pool was closed and
he's grown seven inches.

My son is not fast
and knows he won't win,
but still he competes.

Long arms and legs,
his first event
the individual medley—

fifty yards butterfly,
then backstroke, breaststroke,
freestyle. He forgets

to pull his goggles
over his eyes. They sit
idle on his forehead.

In the bleachers,
I watch him struggle.
By the end of the first lap,

he trails. I wait to see
if he'll quit the race.
I call out his name,

Julian, Go! I know
he can't hear my voice.
He finishes last.

Eyes burning,
he grins up at me.

- Michael Hardin

Playing Football for Jesus

Monday morning, two weeks before school started, and the coach blew the whistle to assemble. My senior year at Maranatha High School, an evangelical school in Sierra Madre, brought a return to the belief that I had as a freshman that football would rescue me from my struggles with masculinity. My dad was the kind of man who could do things with his hands; in high school he built a bedroom set—dresser and bedstead—that he gave my mom as a wedding present. In junior high, I should have failed woodshop, but the teacher had been an usher at Emmanuel with my dad; I couldn't make a simple gravitational bookshelf. And girls: I had never had a girlfriend or even a date. Girls made me nervous; I couldn't talk to them and hoped that if I were on the football team, maybe a girl would come up and talk to me. I was tired of being a nerd, not that I wanted to stop succeeding academically, but I wanted to be accepted. I believed that being on the football team would help me through the trauma of high school.

I had tried football my freshman year, thinking that because I had played flag football at Pasadena Christian in eighth grade, tackle football in high school would not be that different. I went to Hell week, shocked that they would use a swear word to refer to anything other than the Earth's core where Satan and non-Christians were tormented, and suffered through a two-hour morning practice accompanied by a two-hour late afternoon practice. The idea was to get us in shape quickly before the school year began. The worst was the running in place drill, where the coach would whistle and I'd have to drop on my stomach in the hard dirt and do a pushup and then pop back up and keep running. Or maybe worse: being lined up against another player and having to run through him; I could never make it past my opponent. The second week was nearly as bad with just as much running and drills and practice time, just without the scandalous name. One home game late in the season, after going to every practice and not playing a down, Coach Morrison allowed me to be on the receiving team during the kickoff. There was a light drizzle and the ball was shanked straight at me in the middle of the field, bouncing end over end. I fumbled it, the other team shoved me out of the way and recovered possession, and Coach Morrison became livid, "You mother-fucking pussy, take your faggot ass back to the bench and stay there. You're off the receiving team for the rest of the season."

A teammate, Trent, who had attended Pasadena Christian with me and teased me in seventh grade when I said I was not a virgin—I had only heard the word in conjunction with the Virgin Mary, so I assumed virgin meant an unmarried woman who had had a baby—came over to me and offered his support: "What would have happened had you caught that ball? We might have won, and that would ruin our perfect season, 0 and 6." That was the sweetest thing any guy has ever said to me. I laughed through my tears as we commiserated about our crappy team. I did not play another down the rest of the season.

Hell week still shocked me, the name as much as the workouts, but I survived. Now I was taller and faster; instead of trying for the offensive line like I had my freshman year—where I was both too slow and too small—I tried out for defensive back, a less brutal position where I would be responsible for chasing the receivers. I was somewhere between second and third string, so if we were winning by a large number, which was highly unlikely, or being slaughtered, much more likely, I might have a chance to play. I wondered if they knew about my botched kickoff return from freshman year. Sometimes I imagined myself making an interception and returning it for a touchdown despite my suspicion that I would never play.

At the end of the last week of summer practice, the varsity football team took a retreat to Big Bear Lake at a cabin that one of the parents owned. It was meant to be a bonding event between players and coaches that was half Lombardi, half Jesus. The Lombardi half I expected and could tolerate, the bashing together of helmeted heads to emphasize a good play, although no one ever approached me with that honor. But I had made it through the first two weeks of practice, so I was technically a teammate.

After we had served ourselves spaghetti and meatballs, the head coach, Mr. Ireland stood in front of the cabin's stone fireplace. Above him was a mounted buck's head, with large glass eyes staring at us like the eyes of God. The captains, with their paper plates balanced on their laps, sat on the black leather sectional couch, the first-string players on the floor at their feet, the second string off to the sides and behind the couch. I was against the wall. Our coach, who had played college football at BIOLA and had been hired to also teach Bible class, began his football pep talk with a verse from Isaiah: *But they that wait upon the Lord shall renew their strength; they shall mount up with wings as eagles; they shall run and not be weary; and they shall walk and not faint.* I expected this verse; it was on a poster in the weight room—actually an outdoor shed with weight equipment next to it. After two weeks of practices, I had not felt like I had the wings of eagles, nor had I run and not grown weary; I privately rolled my eyes, content that at least I could walk and not faint. Coach Ireland followed Isaiah with Pop Warner and Vince Lombardi, but those references were foreign to me and didn't stick. The only non-Biblical thing that stayed with me was "no pain, no gain"; he talked about it as if it applied in all aspects of one's life, not just exercise—academics, relationships, life in general. With Larry and the church, I had experienced pain, but wasn't sure about what I had gained.

Finally, the pep talk evolved into sports sermon. Coach Ireland chose for his text Ephesians: *Finally, my brethren, be strong in the Lord, and in the power of his might. Put on the whole armor of God, that ye may be able to stand against the wiles of the devil. . . .* The coach compared the various parts of the football uniform to the armor of God. He explained that we when we dressed for football, we should think of our hip pads as girding our loins with truth (I thought the jock strap might be a better translation); our shoulder pads of righteousness; our cleats the preparation of the gospel; our helmets salvation; our arms the sword of the Spirit. Had we been competing against public schools, this metaphor might have made sense, but we were playing other Christian schools in Los Angeles and Orange counties, so the armor of God against the wiles of the evil one seemed a stretch. But again, this was a football coach who had attended a Baptist college, hired primary for his coaching, only secondarily for his ability to teach a Bible class. I wondered if even God could make our team any better, or if our prayers and those from the other Christian football teams simply cancelled each other out, reducing it back to a game of skill, in which case we were in trouble.

Then the team captains spoke, claiming that God gave them their abilities at football (I silently laughed—nothing in the Bible ever suggested that God cared one bit about sports). A second coach, one who taught sophomore Bible, led a prayer asking God to reward us for our hard practices, to protect us from injuries, and to bless our season, promising that we would seek to bring glory to God through our play. Like most evangelical prayers, it was open ended, concluding with a call for those who needed to confess to speak up. These were not conventional sins that we were being asked to confess, but football sins. One of the team captains, the quarterback, was the first to speak up: he was not known for being particularly Christian—I had known him since seventh grade and he was a "pretty jock" and little more. He confessed to not giving 110 percent all the time, and he prayed that Christ would help him to give that magical extra ten percent. Another captain confessed to not always playing as Christ would have played, whatever that meant—maybe not telling parables while making a tackle.

After about half the team had confessed, I felt compelled to as well; the closed eyes of the team made it easier to speak up. But I had no real football sins to confess, except the fumble, since I had never really played football. "Dear Lord, please forgive me for not playing football my sophomore and junior years—I was afraid that I would have to sit on the bench all season or be on the JV team as a junior. Please help me to be the best football player I can be and to serve you in all I do, Amen."

Coach Ireland said, "Good job, Mike," as if I had done something difficult, and announced to the room that it was I who had just spoken. At the same time, I felt a few players around me put their hands on my back as if they were praying for me, but I was feeling nauseous and kept my eyes closed, not wanting to see them stare at me, ashamed that I had publicly confessed to something so stupid. Soon another player started confessing, but I could no longer concentrate and squished myself against the wall.

Once the prayer was over, I went to the room I was sharing with nine other boys and got in my sleeping bag, where I spent the entire night feigning sleep and fighting a massive headache, waiting for the moment when we could drive down the mountain and go home.

The retreat reminded me of what I already really knew: I would not be accepted as an equal member by the team, which in turn would mean no acceptance by the other high school students. My senior year would not make me popular, and most of my graduating class of one hundred would not know who I was. There was nothing to be gained from sitting on the bench for another season of football. I carried my pads, helmet, and uniform to the coaches' office next to the weight shed before practice on the following Monday, the first day of school. All three coaches were there. I placed my gear on the floor of the office and addressed Mr. Ireland, "I've decided not to play."

"You can't quit now, the team depends on you." I knew that he did not believe that, but was applying pressure for me to be a real man.

"I have to," I mumbled.

"Quitting is a sign of weakness."

"I just can't do it."

"I really thought you'd stick with it this time."

"I'm sorry." I turned and walked out.

Coach Ireland whispered to the other two, "I knew he couldn't hack it."

- Michael Hardin

Friends

Brought outside during a dinner party and used for an ash tray years ago,
the empty tomato purée can on the porch has fused the elements

into an object that the eye reconsiders as a piece of found art.
The friends who gathered then are now akin to Eliot's

burnt-out ends of smoky days.
Lives that intersect for a time before they go separate ways.

Cold memento, frozen ash, frost on the rust, a lost face
within the withered wrapper; considered again, just trash.

While listening to the ground beneath the snow breathe,
I also hear from inside the house among those asleep your wheeze.

- Stephen Campiglio

Prayer At Such Times

Bangkok was once covered entirely in canals, you said. To get from one place to another, you took a longtail boat. Everything floated, even the markets. You would eat your bowl of noodles and drink your sweet young coconut as you floated through villages of bamboo huts balanced impossibly on stilts. The chanting of monks, the scent of burning incense, the unbelievable heat. The pink lotus and lily pads blooming everywhere around you. The children swimming naked in the canals crying out Hello, hello! My god, what a thrill it was to be alive!

That was the beginning of your time in war, or close to it. You were the young American soldier on holiday who made the market girls giggle. In your boots and dog tags and fatigue, you entered sparkling temples where their giant golden buddhas and heavens were held, marched up to their altars, and ate the fruits offered to their gods. Shake the box of wooden sticks and see which one spills out, which one spells your fate.

You were stationed on the border, dressed in camouflage, holding a gun nearly the same size as you. Pacing back and forth all day through clouds the color of orange Fanta. Or else wriggling your way through the holes in the earth you yourself had dug. Or else running for your life through a torrential rain in a jungle of buried bombs. Children chopped to pieces, their howling mothers raped and shot. You bled, you bruised, you broke pieces of yourself. And while you were being stitched back together in the make-shift hospital tent, your whole platoon was blown to bits. Silently screaming yourself awake from dreams. But alive!

You came back at night. Your mother in her housecoat and slippers, washing dishes at the kitchen window. Please don't let anything happen to him, she whispered each day to her invisible god. Shrieking when she saw you through the glass, certain it must be your ghost walking up the path. Then – oh! It was her son returned; her son come home! Thinner, older in the eyes, the same though somehow different… But alive!

Years later, dressed in a white linen and a wreath of jasmine, you went with your wife to the same places that hurt you. You met those who'd been hurt too, still lost in their own jungles, you visited those same temples – a lotus bloomed from mud, one hundred whispered offerings. You had killed men, many men, and now those temples held your secret.

You bought a sportscar, had children, read thousands of books, struck up conversation with nearly everyone you met, wandered slim, cobbled streets and entered great cathedrals searching for that same feeling you'd had floating in those canals. You looked for it everywhere.

One winter day, you were already old, you sat in the doctor's office, listening as he spoke your fate. Of the orange clouds at the border that had gone into your breath and into your cells, churning and churning until they'd turned themselves into something else. A small chance with treatment, he told you as your dreams tilted and spun. All of us wanting to keep you here on earth with us even though it might be hell. But alive! But alive!

- Donna Obeid

Local Influencer

You sing until you can only feel your throat, belting into a computer microphone then playing it back, trying to harmonize and sync all the little pieces. This beat's not as tight as the last, but you have a valid excuse. You're brain-dead, running on caffeine and goodwill, uncertain where the week really ends, and all the while pretty sure nobody's going to actually listen.

These words will always mean something, but you're better off just taking another selfie for the base. Almost 9000 now. Try not to focus on how many of them are pervs, swiping on women way too young. You wouldn't have the heart to tell some thirty-year-old asshole they ain't no Leo. Men never hear correctly anyway, but continue to follow out of some misguided fantasy that you're the answer.

Or maybe they're into the whole package: voice, words, beats and boobs. It's not like you're some prude. The greats flaunt it out of necessity. Just a little gloss, a lower watt bulb and that classic bad-girl glare before the flash. Nope, not that one, you blinked. This one makes you look a little too stoned. Something's weird with your upper lip in the next one, and there are too many lines on your forehead in the one after that. Number 28 is the best, but you still have to slap on some filters, maybe fuck around a bit in Photoshop then reupload.

"Yo, sup girl? You around? Think you could do me a favor?" When Buckley texts, your heart ricochets.

It's been awhile since that's happened, and you know why, but aren't ready to admit anything. "Yeah, sure, what's up?"

"Shoot over to my place?"

It's not late enough, just that dark winter you can't accept. Check the bus schedule then consider an outfit, something sexy but warm for the ride. Dab of blush then flip the hair, your best smile in the mirror. That's the picture you should post. In love but nobody really knows it, and whatever they're thinking is only partially correct. That's you in this moment, about to bundle up if only to be closer.

Plug in some buds, groove in the elevator, outside and down the block. Nobody's waiting at the stop. Tonight, it's like an Audrey Hepburn movie, dim blue moonlight shining through cold breath; the bus brakes squeaking in time with electronic bass as you board and nod at the driver. Not much of a crowd, just an old set of thick rims and his lady slurping her big gulp. They ignore you, nerves settling towards the back.

Buckley's been acting too cool since your trip to the shore, strutting with a grin you've never seen on another man. You like how his lips almost touch the tip of the dagger tattoo when he's happy. At first you thought the ornate lines would be a distraction, but you've warmed to them, how Buckley personifies that dangling edge, a knife with just enough shine to draw blood.

You're skittish on the sidewalk, uncertain of what it means to be at his apartment when you have class and work tomorrow. It's only been a day since you've slept together, but the last few times weren't as good as the beach. He's been less present, far from thrilled to hear your ideas and adjust the lenses, to light candles and get the right amount of bubbles in the tub. He was yours and you were his, even if the finished product is for the world. You want them to see you at that moment, the way you look when you're with him.

Buckley answers the door in his puffy orange coat, cap pulled over his eyebrows. He's fidgety, but calm. "Hey…"

"Hey, what's crackin' dawg?" you joke.

"Yeah, so I gotta tell you something."

"Okay."

It's then a knock from inside the apartment. Buckley shrugs, opening the door to reveal a small boy, maybe six, buzzcut and the same faultless expression. He says his name is Curtis, and you're simultaneously thrilled and terrified to meet him. Buckley brushes you into his living room; a handful of action figures intwined on the carpet.

Curtis explains the story as you humor him all the while waiting to adjust. A whole month without a single mention. Who are these two when they're together, and what was it like before you arrived? You let the tension ease back up your spine as Buckley nods, aloof. "But they all fight each other sometimes because they have to," Curtis rambles. "Because sometimes a parasite comes and make ones of them bad for a little while, or all them bad."

"Can I talk to you for a second?" you calmly ask, eyes fixated.

"Okay." Buckley steps to the kitchen. "You just sit tight here a sec, bud. We'll be right back."

You push him in past the fridge and try not to lose your shit. "What the fuck? I can't fucking believe you, that you would hide something like this from me. I mean, I've been in this apartment almost every night for the last two weeks and…"

"Hey listen, I know." Buckley places a hand on your shoulder. "And I'm sorry, but there are bigger things happening right now, and I need to go take care of something."

"What bigger things? What could be more important than being here with your son, and how could you fucking hide him from me?"

"Ya know that producer that came into the club the other night, the one that's worked with everybody who matters?"

"Hansen?"

"Yeah, that's it. Him. Brick shot me a text, said he's been sweet talking him for the last hour, and that if ever there was a time I was gonna front this guy something, now would be it."

"What?"

"Your demo. I'm gonna get it in his hands tonight. I'm gonna make this happen for the both of us. I finished the video we shot, and now is the right time, biatch."

Your heart sinks as he smiles and you try not to. "This can't be happening."

"I'm gonna make it happen, but I need you to stay here with Curtis, because I can't, and I promise I'll explain all of this later, but you and I both know that you only get so many moments like this, and when they come, ya gotta take 'em, and that's what I'm doing for us, okay?"

You love him and know that this is an instant you'll talk about for the rest of your lives. "Okay, go. Lock this shit down."

"Damn girl, I love you." He wraps his mitts around your cheeks and his lips feel cold for the first time.

"Yeah, I know."

"And just think about it. This is the perfect opportunity for the two of you to get to know each other without me screwing it up."

"Yeah, that's your thing, isn't it?" You want to burn a hole in his skull.

"Look, I gotta skedaddle, but I'll be back soon as I can, and hell, we'll go to the zoo tomorrow or something, just don't tell Curtis, because I want it to be a surprise."

"I'll keep it on the D.L."

"Cool, he already knows I gotta go, so just play nice, alright?" Buckley beams.

"You know it."

You follow him as he pats the kid and dips out the door. Curtis immediately hops up from the floor. "Can we watch wrestling?"

"Um…sure. Is it on?" you ask.

"It's always on. Let's watch it." Curtis grabs the remote and starts to flip as you fall back on the couch, immediately lost in the folds. He talks at you for a good hour, but eventually loses steam. There's no second bedroom, so you walk him to Buckley's air mattress, noticing he hasn't changed the sheets in a week. This isn't a place for a child, which makes you consider your approach. You should ask about his mother or the past six years, but instead let Curtis drone about heroes and villains until he passes out.

Netflix, but you doze off; the sun shining in early. Your eyes blink to find Curtis aloof in the threshold. "I wet the bed again."

"Oh, well…that's okay," you gargle, sitting up. "I used to do that all the time freshman year."

"I'm hungry too."

"Well um…Is your dad not home?"

"He said he won't be home for a long time?"

"What? When did he say that?"

"Last night. He was putting all of his clothes in a bag while I ate my ice cream cone."

Now you're awake, finding your legs as they pull you into the bedroom. The closet is bare and so are his dresser drawers; empty emergency-fund shoebox and no condoms in the nightstand. The revolver and his laptop, camera and cellphone charger; all seemingly more important than his girlfriend. You play it all back and then start to cry, collapsing and slobbering into your sleeve.

It's the sound a phone makes when it takes a picture; that old familiar shutter as you roll over to Curtis pointing the lens. "Can you call your mom for me? I'm gonna try and get a hold of your dad."

"I don't know my mom," the child replies. "This is dad's phone. Why are you sad?" You consider the situation like it's a bad sitcom. "I'll post these for you. They're really funny pictures."

You stand and snatch the phone from Curtis, checking the contact list. Only two numbers: yours and Brick's. He hasn't seen him. This was a life left behind, and you can't help but feel empty, like when you finally figure out who unfollowed your feed for no reason whatsoever.

- Christopher Bell

134

In Which I Unthinkingly Meet the Eye of a Homeless Woman in the Park

She screams at me, but I would scream at me
and have for a similar nothing, just for looking,
my eyes meeting hers. *What are you staring at?!*
she shrieks, sensing rightly my assessing, the implicit
judgment—*Poor thing!* She would have my head
if she could. I pick up my pace, resisting the urge

to glance backwards over my shoulder, the urge
of Lot's wife. *Who would even notice me?*
she thought as her body stiffened, toe to head.
That's the danger—that you'll be caught looking,
your face an open book. We bare the implicit
like a tattoo. So what school did *you* study at?

Not subtle. We know what we're getting at—
family connections, resources, the shameful urge
to one up. The madwoman accepted the implicit
challenge. I'd do the same if it were me—
scream until every last walker were looking
my direction. Did you know a severed head

continues to think? Imagine such a head
processing its demise. Imagine the panic. At
what point is it resigned, or does it keep looking
until all blood has leaked away, the urge
outlasting its engine, the *I* clinging to its *me*
until the last drained vein collapses? Implicit

is the regret, the grief, the indignation, implicit
the critique that the material world dominates the head.
Promise me reincarnation. Swear to me
that the next life will be more just. The woman at
the drinking fountain, screaming, is resisting the urge
to do even greater damage—to kill me for looking.

My students testing, I kill time looking
at a rare snake choked by a centipede. Implicit
is the message of self-control. Your every urge
can lead to this, to swallowing more than your head

can process—the echo: What are you looking at?
Lady, not at *you!* I'm looking at *me!*

Chagrined, I cease looking and bow my head.
Implicit is a plea for transcendence, for arriving at
the dissolution of every urge, an *Ah hah!* filling me.

- Devon Balwit

All Heart and No Legs

I left a goodbye note with my whereabouts and escape route in the Calvin and Hobbes book next to the downstairs toilet.

Calvin and Hobbes have all the answers, I said, heading to the door and avoiding any eye contact.

They sure do, he said, not looking up as I walked out the door, never to see him again.

Earlier that day, I kissed him and he sort of let me in an "I hate this" way, which was actually way better than usual. A sudden improvement that made me doubt my entire plan. I considered ditching the whole thing because of a meh kiss. *Maybe he forgot to hate me just then.* Normally, he would make a grimacing face, dramatically wipe off the kiss, or shove me away. If he was feeling lazy, he would simply lift his head up so high that I couldn't reach his lips because he was a foot taller than me.

His mouth tasted like potato chips that morning. Potato chips tasted like settling. I'd never liked the taste of greasy, standard potato chips but now when I have one, it tastes even more like a lazy, lazy lie.

After this penultimate peck, I went upstairs like a good wife to wash out his jockstrap, wring it out, and hang it on the towel hanger. He had just gotten circumcised three days earlier. It was a calculated murder-of-a-marriage. He had been stabbing it for a long, long while but only in the arms and legs.

My husband was on day 3 of a medical order to not have sex for six weeks, or even get a hard-on if he could help it (with depo-provera to serve that end). Hell, if there was any time that I could leave the love of my life without bashing my head into a glass counter every time I imagined who he was doing on that island, then it would be then. Every woman dreams of cutting the dick off a man who has lied to her. Most women don't get to have their dream performed by a Naval doctor.

I'm going to work, I said, wearing shorts and standing in the doorway. No matter what the weather on The Island was, you still walked out the door and were covered in your own sweat in a matter of minutes. I am anxious while wearing sweaters. I've sweated through my clothes on every one of the therapy phone calls I've had for the last fifteen years. But on that morning, I did not sweat an ounce, I was totally and completely dry.

***

I had followed him to The Island even though it seemed like we were getting divorced. I wanted to be the one who moved across the world with him, for the sake of it. He had always done things for the sake of them, for no other reason than that they felt good for a good few seconds, not considering the consequences or long-term effect. That was what I idolized about him. And that was more than enough to live off till the next delusion.

If I was wise, I would have asked for a temporary separation while he

137

was stationed there and started my career in New York City. Space to think is a good thing. But clinging felt better than being wise. Also, it is impossible to be wise when you don't know *wise options.* My mother told me a story once of her hugging a Guinea Pig so tightly as a child that she killed it. I think it runs in the family. If I had known wise options, I would have packed up the moment he started being mean, but I squeezed the life out of that marriage instead. We did sign up for a marriage retreat once. It was scheduled the same weekend the hotel had booked a high school cheerleading convention though, so it really wasn't all that helpful.

***

We were told there were no birds on The Island, which was weird because on day one, we saw a bird. I think it was Christmas Eve. Seeing a bird upon your arrival when you have just prepared yourself to not see a bird for years is rather hopeful. Maybe there would also be love in a marriage where there wasn't any. Not only were there birds, but the water was, unlike my mind, a calm clear teal.

Meat-On-A-Stick was something to look forward to on Tuesdays on The Island. They had a community market with the locals, giving the Navy families something to do. I never touched the Meat-On-A-Stick, or the Spam ... or the Tang. But now I wish I had. I was too busy on the phone with my therapist trying to figure out what to do about Jack. So much for marrying a man who makes you feel like you are in the present, and not learning how to make yourself feel like that.

Things were not good but at the same time, they were absolutely wonderful, like many happy/sad relationships.

***

One nice day on The Island, we went on three different top recommendation adventures. One long hike with crosses at the summit, a waterfall, an especially gorgeous, empty beach. I was trying to pack it all in at once because I knew I was leaving soon. We took Polaroids with real Polaroid film.

I felt vibrant, special, and young, but when I look at the photos now, it seems I needed a fashion upgrade, and that I was just regular. I held onto Jack on the back of his motorcycle and spurred around The Island. I listened to Sharon Van Etten and began writing my own songs, songs I would later sing at clubs, for my third-charm try, my prodigal return, to New York City.

***

As I wrote the note at the kitchen counter he asked his video game screen, *When will you be back?*

He had the voice of someone who had smoked for a very long time, and the attitude of someone who had done shrooms and acid for a very long

138

time. Once he did shrooms for 30 days straight. I think he left himself back there somewhere staring into the mirror and watching his face coagulate into a silk curtain.

The truth was that I was not going to be back for a very long time, and, in fact, that I would never see him again. I did something I don't do often in life. I lied. *A few hours. Can I borrow your guitar?*

Yeah, he said, without looking away from the screen. Without wondering why the hell I'd be borrowing the guitar. I didn't play guitar, he did. But it was a symbol of the life to come: a singer-songwriter in New York City. Alone, playing her way through the streets. It was not cool enough to just leave The Island without telling anyone. I needed to leave with his guitar on my back. Who was I kidding. I could only play five chords. It was my way of taking him with me.

His response was handy because I already had packed the guitar and one single suitcase in the trunk the night before.

I said, *I love you,* and he said nothing. I think. It's hard to remember. Maybe he said I love you that time, just to fuck with me, or out of loose habit. Maybe for some reason, he didn't hate me that morning, or felt bad because he knew I knew about the lies.

I drove to the airport. Parked the car. Hid the keys under the mat. And flew, first to Japan, then to San Francisco with the ticket my dad got for me. Sometimes, when you tell someone to disappear every day for years, they finally do.

***

The week before, I had gone and gotten nude photos with my wedding ring on. I met with a woman in a hotel room, and she told me to pose in certain ways. I remember thinking that everyone was getting the same pictures in the same poses, and how dumb that was. I wore lots of makeup and fake eyelashes, and even hair extensions. I wore lingerie I'd never worn before. I brought his guitar there too.

A few nights after discovering the lies, I placed the printed-out book of photos of myself on the toilet seat. I told him to go upstairs and look at them.

He came down and said that he did more than look at them. He asked me if this was to get back at him.

I told him that most women would probably not give their husbands a book of naked photos of them after being hurt so much, but that I was not most women. He said it was a weird flex and even stranger revenge move. He did not say he loved me for being so weird or that I had a better figure than anyone else. He told me which photo he liked best and then told me I wasn't a lady. I couldn't be one if I tried. I didn't even wear heels. I was a lady fraud.

***

I had been afraid of planes at some point, but the one from The Island was hard to get on, for different emotional reasons and lonelier earth-bound fears. I looked out at the bluesy water of The Island and thought, *This is not a place you return to; this is a final goodbye.*

I didn't think to myself that I would never see him again. Had I been mature enough to say goodbye back then, I would have. But I was all heart and no legs and would have stayed forever if I had to confront our ending face-to-face.

***

I scheduled the departure after closing night. I was cast in a show where I got to wear a cute dress and hang with a hot Island guy. I watched his muscular, island-kissed back during a costume change as he took his shirt off over his head. He asked me every night if he could button up my dress. Of course, I was perfectly able to button up my dress, and I think he knew that. But maybe he sensed how bad things were when I got home after the show each night. I wondered if his relationship was also a pumpkin and not a carriage.

During this production, in a write-up, a newspaper reporter mainly focused on how stunning I was. The world of my entire young life was falling apart, and it felt lovely for someone to notice me. If this were a corny movie, I would say that what he wrote about me in that paper helped give me the strength to leave and made me see my own value.

I sat at a desk where I ran a magazine and an Etsy store. I was interviewing women like Sophie Blackall and other artists from Chicago. I read his article and felt a lifeline just morphed into existence like lightning in the forest that passes so close to you that you were blinded for a second. You look to see a ponderosa pine struck down the center, burning away like a candle. It somehow burns safely on the rim of a canyon. The love I needed was on this island, but could I find him? I looked him up.

Impossible ghost to find, I found him years later, although I could never find the article again. He was older, had a son, and was maybe married but getting divorced. I couldn't tell.

But the truth is that my husband's late-onset dick snip takes center stage credit. It provided the perfect window of opportunity for someone as territorial as me to escape through. He wouldn't be fucking any island girls for six weeks, and I'd care less by then. Or, more likely, be too far away to do anything illegal about it.

At that point, I still only intended to separate and work things out later. He was the one who wanted me to leave, and I was doing him a favor by orchestrating the whole deal without any drama.

I liked doing him favors. So, I ordered him a burger delivered to the house from the plane, and he sent me a text message that said, "I understand why you are doing this," and, "Thank you." I didn't realize he would have used the bathroom and read that note so quickly. I thought it could have been weeks. People have to use the bathroom, I suppose. He asked where the car was. I politely told him where it was and where the keys were, and from a flip

140

phone, every letter had to be pressed two or three times.

During the 12-hour flight, I thought about how I chose a lot of hurt over half a marriage. I had the rest of my life and the middle row to myself on the first leg of the flight. After surviving take off, I wrote down my feelings on the back of an envelope, the only paper I had. I only had one feeling: help. So I wrote only one sentence. It said: "There is a way. I cannot yet see it."

***

A few months earlier, Jack tried to end all my worries about whatever was to happen with us with a motorcycle helmet, pinning me against a wall with the helmet. I always thought he looked so handsome on that bike. A few seconds earlier, I had hugged him goodbye and felt the photo album, the one with pictures of his actual high school sweetheart, who wasn't me, making a bulge in his backpack. I realized he had chosen old photos of his 16-year-old ex to serve him while serving our country on deployment. I let this void me of all value, all matter. My many fears were confirmed. I was the wife, not the secret bulge. I knew the photos were in there because I had snooped around in what looked like a to-be-packed pile the night before, but I wasn't sure. I had never seen them before and was disgusted. Would he pack them, I wondered? I could have thrown them out that night. I wish I had. But I was too curious to see what he planned to do with them. Too bent on catching him in the act.

So, by the front door, I tried to physically get those photos from him, as if my desperate attempt would make my husband be attracted to me instead of a child. Suddenly, I was not just in a fight for my very pride, my sexual worth, and my dignity as a woman and wife, but a fight for my life.

In the end, those photos got thrown away after he, embarrassed, realized that he had actually tried to kill me over them. I, also embarrassed, realized I could have died over something so sad and stupid. I could have died for no cause at all, only the cause of not being able to bear my now-adult-husband imagining cumming all over the body of a not-adult-girl.

Who needs photos of a kid, Jack? I stressed. *A kid. You were both children back then. She's an adult now,* I lectured him. *At least get some recent photos of her to keep it legal. Facebook exists. Use it,* I said.

I was distraught that he would choose her naked body over mine to jack off to, but I still wanted to sound logical and smart, having survived the incident. Forgetting that my life had just been at the mercy of his embarrassed rage and perversion, I dove right back in—digging into his pride with the moral knife of my words as soon as I could breathe.

***

Jack locked me in a room during a party that I had planned for him and his friends. His friends had moved to The Island from Sametown, and I wanted them to come to our place. Jack let me plan this party and then locked me upstairs while I heard him make jokes with his friends. Eventually, I fell asleep, very sad after texting him angrily that he didn't even let me serve the pie.

After a while, he stopped coming home. It isn't uncommon to sleep alone on The Island and wake up without your husband next to you. Many navy wives woke up to empty beds because their husbands were deployed. Mine was just partying on the same island as me, probably passed out drunk, and had taken the car. While their husbands were away, mine was away in a very different sense.

We fought so hard. I was scared one of us would kill the other. There was a lot of passion in everything that we did. There was passionate pushing, shoving, and screaming, and we never went one night without sex. I must have had a lot more energy back then for it all. A pregnant neighbor complained. After that, we lowered our arguments' pitch, decibel, and volume for a bit. Then we both wondered if maybe she wasn't pregnant and just used that as an excuse to make us feel guilty. So we started up at full volume again.

***

Approaching land after flying over water for a really long time, I felt strongly reminded that the ocean and tropics just weren't for me. I had learned this a few years prior when I was in Costa Rica for my first semester of college. The humidity and heat were no friends of mine. I was raised in a xeric, landlocked state with no water access, and dry land was comforting and stable.

Maybe the California coast would do my parents well. Perhaps access to water was all that failed marriage needed. My mother loved the water, and my father loved messing around with my mother. It was no surprise that they had gotten back together after the divorce, but the fact that they did so in San Francisco intrigued me. I had never really been there before for much time. When I arrived, it was bucolic; the spring made it temporarily half-frozen and half blooming, just like me. It was a perfect setting to heal in, besides hearing my parents have rabid, post-divorce sex upstairs while I had just run away from having to get one.

I immediately ended up in a hot tub with my favorite musician who invited me to join him on tour to Chicago. With long brown hair and 0% body fat, he told me that life is just one long goodbye party. I fell for him as hard as any divorce escapee can. After my first sexual experience since my marriage, he canceled the invitation the week before we were going to leave because he was in love with someone else, too. He was wrong about inviting me on tour. He was right, though, about the goodbye party thing.

I guess I'm like that girl next door who sheds light on the fact that you are in love with the girl down the street. I hoped maybe one day I could be the girl down the street. Maybe you only get to be the girl down the street for a little while.

***

A few days before the divorce, Jack said, *You know I married you for the mon-*

142

ey, right?

But I was used to seeing through the mean things people said when they wanted to hurt you. When do tender-hearted feelings get replaced with cruelty and the opposite? When the dance ends. When the color of one seeps so far into the other that it becomes another color completely.

When I look at pictures now of him, I see us lying on top of each other at the four corners. I see he is laying over me, which is strange. Then I think about who took the picture. I remember my tripod. I see his abdomen, below his belly button. It is so flat. It looks like one of our kids. It isn't a dad bod. It isn't a beer belly. His stomach was so lean. How is it that I did not even notice that his stomach was so lean.

***

So, after moving to San Francisco and staying with my parents, I did what any self-respecting, almost divorcee at the age of twenty-three would do, I became a band groupie.

Or almost. I almost became a band groupie.

- Katie King

The Hair on the Wall of the Shower

It's mine. It always is.
Much too long to be someone else's.
It's patterns
on the wall
always bemuse me.
I could make a painting
out of that shape,
I think.
But then I sit down
at a desk and no art comes out.
So nothing is done
about the hair on the wall in an interesting shape.
It stays there until tomorrow's shower.
Washed away.
A new hair sprouts in its place to taunt me.

- Amanda Huffman

Anatomy of the United States of America

I read once that Janis Joplin called her home town
The armpit of Texas, and I thought that a little rough.
I imagined her standing on stage in a dark, smoky nightclub
In the liberal heart, the state capital of Austin,
Throwing off an aura of sandpaper, her voice gritty like granola underfoot.

But the armpit never struck me as rancid
Unless one let the hair grow like brill weeds
Or failed to clean and apply deodorant
A minor erotic zone, really.

And I wondered what other poor cities were defined as
Less than wondrous parts of the human form;
What town would be the second knuckle from the end,
The little hairs that grow from the ears,
The wrinkled skin of an elbow or the sunburned scalp?

Is there a Uvula, Montana and Xyphoid, Iowa?
The Isles of Langerhans resting in the fog just off coast of Maine?
How rough is the rugged terrain of Wrinkly Knee, North Dakota,
And how slick and damp and wet is Sinus, Alabama?

I think of New York City and Los Angeles as the eyes
Like a chameleon's, turning this way and that, watching to the east and west.
Chicago, the mouth, roaring and brash, or open wide in a great yawn.
And New Orleans, the feet, rising and sliding to some slinky jazz
Or shuffling across the sawdust to some sizzling zydeco.

- James Mathis

145

Boy Trouble

For the first time in years, no one knew where I was. My husband Stephen thought I was at the dentist. I wasn't. I was on the 405 freeway on the way to meet my ex-boyfriend Len at a Middle Eastern restaurant in Burbank. It was a Friday in September. Stephen was working at his office in Hollywood about five miles away; our son Jade was, no doubt, getting into trouble at his swanky private school near our home in Manhattan Beach. I kept visualizing my family as coordinates on a map, measuring our proximity to one another. The farther I got from them, the more anxious I became.

My body felt warm, too warm. Almost feverish. Sweat was forming under the uber-padding of my new underwire bra. Lingerie as cutlery: dug in and served up. The ratio of breast to material was not good math. It felt as if a small animal was sitting between me and my shirt. Worse was the thong I wore—the Marquis de Sade of underwear. It had been hibernating in my butt since I got into the car. I tried once to lift myself and pull it out, but within seconds it had stubbornly resumed its position. Really, it oughtn't be sold as underwear. Sex toy—weapon, perhaps.

A voice inside me shouted, *What are you doing?*

I gripped my hands at 11:00 and 1:00 but answered calmly: *Nothing. Just lunch.*

Then why did you buy new underwear? This other voice was tougher, meaner than me. A bully living in my head, the same one that tempted me to say inappropriate things to other mothers or tell my husband's boss what he really thought of him.

A number of red cars clustered around me, a coincidence I found conspiratorial. The Santa Monica Mountains grew taller as I drove north. I felt stalked by them. The sky turned a purplish-blue, like a bruise, and a black sedan tailgated me. I accelerated to ninety. Within a mile, a policeman pulled me over with a single shriek of a siren that I swore sounded like "SLUT!" My hands shook as I handed him my license and paperwork. I released short puffs of air that smelled like Crest and acid reflux. I hadn't eaten breakfast.

The policeman leaned over my car, looked around. "Know why I stopped you?"

Because you had a controlling father who made you feel weak so you got this job to prove that you're not?

I shook my head.

"Ninety in a sixty-five." He thrust his holster-bearing hips forward. "Be right back."

Traffic slowed and heads turned. My eyes felt cool inside my hot skin.

I turned away. The hillside next to me was barren and brown, ripe for a forest fire. Trash had collected in the gutter, between hill and highway. Litter was my pet peeve. I imagined myself out of the car, spearing trash. I wondered if that would win me points with the policeman. Why not bypass the middleman—go straight from moving violation to public service? Already, I'd constructed an anecdote in my head to tell Len. The policeman returned, said something that I didn't hear, and shoved the ticket in my unsteady hand.

I put on a CD to calm myself down—Radiohead, because I imagined Len would admire me for that choice. When he'd called, I immediately recognized his voice, as though only a week had passed instead of ten years. "I'm sorry. Can you hold on one second?" I had this habit of wanting to guess things before someone told me. LEN BEDARD REALIZED YOU WERE THE LOVE OF HIS LIFE, AFTER ALL! I was in my kitchen making a list of my son's therapies for the week. Jade has ADHD, or as I call it, "boy syndrome." In case you haven't been around young boys in the last fifteen years or so, there's this new movement against boys who act like boys that may have been started by underpaid teachers and older parents, like me—people who'd spent too many years lingering in restaurants, seeing foreign films and other carefree activities to adapt to their child's frenetic energy. Under occupational therapy, social skills, neuro-feedback, and the rest of Jade's therapies, I wrote Len's name like a high school girl would. I imagined Stephen seeing Len's name and quickly turned the "L" into a boot.

I'd set the phone down and had a fake conversation with my son who was at therapy three miles away because, after all, Len had left me and I didn't want to appear like I cared about that.

"I'll be right there to help you Jade, okay?"

Pause.

"Okay?!" I said louder, like I might have if Jade were really there. "I'm sorry. Who's calling?"

"Len. Len Bedard." His voice was soft. What I remembered about Len was this: you could barely hear him outside of bed. In bed, he was louder than any man I'd ever been with, as if his penis was connected to his vocal cords.

"Len? Hi. How *are* you?"

The cat walked in, looked at me, and narrowed his eyes. I turned away. You never knew, in the grand scheme of things, if animals were in on it.

Len told me his mother had died.

"Oh, Len. I'm so sorry." I heard him sigh, long. More things about him were coming back to me. He spoke slowly, deliberately. Time was irrelevant. I checked my watch. In five minutes, I had to fetch Jade from his appointment. I didn't want to make Len feel like I was dismissing him so I said, "Hey, I'm coming over your way next week to go to the dentist."

"You still go to that same dentist?"

"I like him," I said, though I really only continued to go because the neighborhood reminded me of Len.

"Lucky for me."

After we hung up, I sprinted out the door. Len's phone call had made me late. Jade's therapist looked at her watch when I arrived at 3:04. She told me how kids like Jade needed structure and routine and stability and schedule. Normally, I would have been bothered, but instead, I semi-saluted, said, "See you Wednesday at 1500 hours," then marched with Jade, "hut two, three, four," to the car.

Jade latched onto my impromptu army sergeant game mock-shooting small objects against the window. I went along until the remnants of his lunch sandwich landed—thwack, dribble—on the dash. I pulled a baggie from my purse and tossed it to him. "War is over. Now we rebuild the land."

Jade grabbed the baggie, blew it up, popped it, yelled "A direct hit!" He formed a gun with his fingers, made machine gun noises and shouted, "It's not over yet, Killface!" then reached over to grab a handful of goldfish crackers, and tossed them one by one across the car, making explosion sounds. "You're dead! You're dead again, suc-ker!"

The clock stopped for me in these moments. His aggressiveness stunned me every time. Often, I lost my temper. In other words, my reactions had as little control as his actions. Still, on that day, Len's call had inserted something protective between me and the world, like the screen that separates cabdrivers from passengers.

"Do you know what happens in times of peace?" He shook his head and cast his eyes up at me. I handed him a box of Legos that I had planned to give away because they were the larger kind for ages 2-4, but would do in a pinch. "You build more weapons."

Jade continued to stare at me, as if to confirm that I was really his mother. Then he took the Legos without another sound.

***

Café Med seated only twenty, and you had to walk through the kitchen, past the gurgling deep fryers with falafels floating on top, to use the restroom. A balding man in a hairnet with a unibrow tended to the falafels. His brow could use the hairnet more, I thought. The air smelled like cooked lamb and oil. After wiping off my sweat and, pointlessly, pulling the thong out of my butt, I walked unsteadily to a table. I sat down and got my book from my bag. A dark-haired man sat alone staring at his fork. When I'd first walked in, I thought he might be Len simply because of the way he sat. Like me, Len leaned against things—posts, people. Gravity was antagonistic. But unless I had never noticed that Len had acne scars, it wasn't him.

Len was my last lover, before I married Stephen. As often happens with consecutive lovers, they were opposites. Stephen's religion was self-discipline. He rarely missed a day of exercise, never touched butter, and folded his clothes before sex. And Stephen would never go to a daytime movie. Ever. Like me, Len was an artist; a cartoonist by trade, with a self-effacing sense of humor. We'd met at Hanna Barbera and slept together after his character—an evil egret—ate mine, a Buddhist monkfish. Len took anti-depressants. His father had committed suicide. He also painted an abstract nude of me, one that hangs in my office. Everyone asks about it. "Yes, I was the kind of woman that once inspired great art," I had joked with friends. Stephen had laughed, "Hey, I got the painting and the girl." This was what had first attracted me to Stephen. His fuck-you attitude towards jealousy.

I thought about the two of them as I sat waiting for Len, feeling the deficits of my attention, like Jade; reading but not reading my book. I kept looking up. The door had one of those high-pitched bells—the pretext of friendliness—that dinged every time someone walked in.

The sun outside seemed almost violent in its insistence on shining. Cooked cars lined the street. A guy wearing boots and an overcoat with alarmed looking hair, as if it had just exited a ski hat, walked in and smiled at me. If I squinted my eyes, and I did, he might have been Len. Something had changed, his looks or my memory. Either seemed probable.

"Trixie?" he said in a thick New York accent, the kind that wasn't going anywhere.

"No." I was annoyed. Seriously, did I look like a Trixie? Had I overdone it with the eyeliner? I went back to impersonating a person not preoccupied with waiting.

Another five minutes, then ding, in he walked. A young boy Jade's age. He was with his mother, a woman who might have played me in the movie version of me. Things like this happened in Burbank. She sat the boy down, pulled out a pack of crayons and kissed him on the cheek. "Be right back, sweetie. I need to use the potty." I held my breath, watching him sit, staring at his crayons. "Mommy?" He looked up. By then his mother stood so close to my table, I could have stuck out my foot and tripped her. She turned back. "Yes?"

"Don't leave me," he said.

Sometimes, moments are doors; other times, they're windows. Problem is, when Len called, I'd mistaken a window for a door; one where Stephen and Jade had no key. On my way out, I checked around for a camera, just to be sure.

Later that night, I sat painting with Jade. His lips were pursed, his grip firm. In between each tank he colored, he leaned over to kiss me. Whenever he'd had a hard day, Jade clung to me like this, as if to ward off whate-

149

ver demons his behavior stirred up. He always painted the same thing: tanks, soldiers, war scenes. I sat watching him for a while. Then I myself started painting. Before I realized it, I'd colored a self-portrait. Jade said, "You look crazy. Like me." I stared at him, and he stared at me. It was a rare thing, eye contact with Jade. I can't explain it, or probably even draw it, but something about that stare was hilarious. We both laughed so hard, we could have made a watercolor with our tears.

- Linda Davis

This Morning I Woke Up in Another Country

Another night of half-sleep at my aunt's. Ninety-five and still going strong. Our care for her is solid, reliable. Its regularity keeps my husband and me grounded.

"Is that tea, dear?" She asks as I approach with her morning draught in a cup, a spoon with white powder in my other hand. "What is that?" She asks, eyeing the powder suspiciously as if this is her first encounter.

"It's your morning pill."

"I hate my pills." They are jagged, she thinks, sure that they will tear apart her throat.

Her smile and her cornflower doe-eyes raise my spirits. An easy morning is on its way.

I look around her room: cosmopolitan circa 1965. She was born in Paris between the wars, grew up in London. As the Stukas warmed their engines for the Blitz, her parents shipped her, my mother, and their sister to the States. I motion to the spoon again. My aunt stares at it, hesitating.

"Lick your finger and stick it in the powder. Then lick it again and take a sip of your tea," I explain. She appreciates the guidance every time.

This is the woman who cried when I came out to her. This is the woman who comforted me when my mother was drinking. This is the woman who brought the wildest Christmas gifts of art-splashed t-shirts and handed out stuffed animals and striped, bug-eyed lemur toys to children and their unsuspecting parents. Her presence is always joy.

She pauses, staring at her hand.

"Your nails need new polish," I say. She loves a visit to the salon. She is sure she is still the seventeen-year-old beauty who captured every gentleman's attention.

"Are we in Paris, dear?"

I try not to show my surprise at this bomb. "No. San Francisco. You moved here to be with your husband. He's gone now."

"Right, yes. Thank you."

"You were born in Paris, though, so you're not far off." I try to reassure her. Or is that reassurance for me? The recent memory of my mother forgetting the easy route for a walk to the elevator taps me on my shoulder. It was the first noticeable sign of her dementia.

My aunt sits there, stalled, staring at her fingers splayed out before her, not reaching toward the spoon.

I feel a slight quiver in my chest. "Why the hesitation?" I ask.

"Hold on a moment," she says. "I'm just trying to figure out which finger is mine."

My eyes wide open. I am awake, my ears alert. Not far off, engines rev. This was the day the assault began.

And now, today, just past her ninety-seventh, freed from body and mind, she has her hands back. And Paris is there with open arms.

- Anthony St George

The Poems of Our Climate

I
Floating in the still water of a stagnant pool:
Gold and brown leaves. The light
Under the trees, flecked with snow,
Reflects in the creek: a snow
At the end of autumn when evening
Starts soon after lunch.
Gold and brown leaves-- did I
Expect more? The season itself is
Reduced to the elemental: a white crust
Of snow, cold air, leafless trees,
Towering canyon walls, the rock streaked with ice,
The creek, with nothing more
Than gold and brown leaves floating there.

II
Could the elemental erase my doubts,
Boil down my intrusive sense of self,
Make myself new in a drift of snow,
In a pool of stagnant water?
Should I desire more, need more,
Than a canyon of white snow?

III
There will be no end to consciousness,
No cessation of the nostalgia
To be myself. The canyon, me--
The lack of completion is our perfection.
I sense the incompletion within me as a desire:
Its cure found in the awesome flaw of relationship:
The smell of stagnant water and crusty snow,
The sight of gold and brown leaves floating
under the shadow of rock streaked with ice

- Benjamin Green

Octopuses and Old Age

God must have run out of steam after he finished making the animals.
Lost his focus. Or maybe he was rushing, wanting to sip Mai Tais on
Miami's sandy beaches, leering at bikinied blondes with big breasts. Not
many spare parts left in his stack. After all, he had given the Octopus nine
brains and three hearts. What a waste. What we wouldn't give for nine
brains so we have backups for when we start losing it. Too many amyloid
plaques and tau tangles. That's what they say. We wander down
unfamiliar streets and forget if we have eaten lunch. We find a stenchy
carton of milk in the hall closet. Instead we could put another brain in
charge. And another after that. But, God, it's the three hearts that hurt the most.
What were you thinking when you gave humans only one heart.
What of a heart attack watching Jack Nicholson in *The Shining?* Or a
shattered heart when Samantha tells us she is so done and is going to study
Sanskrit in Deli. Or ride a raft around the South Pole. You know you
wasted valuable resources on this short-lived cephalopod. I swallow your
wafers, drink your wine and pray the next time you will do a better job.
That's what I say.

- Claire Rubin

I Think I Know Why I Am Afraid

Imagine a seven-year-old in the most hyperbolic state: disproportioned like an oversized toddler, trembling weakly, giggling at the discomfort of it all. I stand in the empty gap of my living room between the love seat and the kitchen floor, fists raised in a weak fighting stance that my father slaps out of position. I'm not strong enough to hold it even if I tried. I still call him Daddy here. He kneels in front of me in his work pants caked in dried mud and grass stains. He's teaching me how to fight.

"Don't put your thumbs in your fist," he orders and takes my hands. "You'll break them that way."

I move my thumbs, bending them awkwardly in front of my four tight fingers. They keep fighting to go back inside my closed hand and retreat like a turtle. I'm laughing—at myself, at my focused father down on my level. The light from the glass door behind him makes his outline glow.

"Stop laughing," he says, "if you're not going to take this seriously, we're not going to do it."

I repress my laughter but not the smile. I try to be tough: narrow my eyes, hunch my shoulders, tense my arms to protect my tiny square chest. Dad spreads my knees with his hands, grabbing my calves to reposition. He looks me in the eyes and puts his arms behind his back.

"Hit me," he says.

My heart drops and my limbs go cold. "What? No!"

"I mean it," he says. "Hit me. I want to see how you punch. You won't get in trouble."

I bounce on my heels, trying to amp up some sort of energy to hit him. I'm faking it. My hands feel foreign, balled up to the point where the muscles in the tops of them are twitching. My hands aren't supposed to feel like this. This is all wrong. I hit Daddy lightly in the chest and spring back, giggling even louder than before. We've been at this for twenty minutes.

"We're done," he says. He climbs up from the floor, stabilizing himself on the back of the couch. He towers over me in his steel-toed boots that I used to stand on, in his Carhart jacket that he used to swaddle me in when Santa Claus came through the neighborhood on a firetruck, in all his power and protective glory. I've failed.

"Are you mad at me?" I ask through the kind of tears only a child truly terrified of disappointing her parents can make.

I press my hands into my face, curled fists on my own cheeks. It's a safety mechanism, pressure on my face. Sometimes it's a blanket curled up under my head with one eye pressed in the fabric or a stuffed animal laid over my eyes to block out the light of the room. Now, it's my hands in perfect form, comforting instead of attacking.

"I'm not mad at you," he says and pulls me into his side as I cry. "I just need you to be able to protect yourself."

This is a cycle we'd spin a dozen times as I got older, and it always ends with that sentiment. He still grapples me, binds my arms behind my back with his hands, and begs me to hit him back. Fight back. Do something. Do something to prove that I am not just a sweet, soft thing for the world to devour. He bought me a black metal ring to wrap around my weak, pointless fist when I was twelve. He convinced me to keep it because it had two triangles on the top that made the whole contraption look like a cartoonish cat outline. He bought me pepper spray when I was sixteen and walking home from school along the highway. He bought me a flashlight with a secret taser function when I moved away to college in New York, one of two states where possession of a taser is illegal under all circumstances.

I carry these weapons apprehensively now. I've never used them, and if the opportunity arises where their presence is necessary, I don't know that I will be able to wield them and live with the relentless guilt that follows.

Confession: I've held a boy's throat in my hands and thought about crushing it. I was eleven. He was eight. He had his fingers around my little brother's neck and turned him purple, so I did it back. I pressed into the boy's chest with my knees and held his thick, throbbing throat. I knew what I was doing. I wish I regretted it. The first step in self-defense is believing you're worth defending. I'll kill for my family, I've discovered, but I don't know if I would do it for myself.

***

Shelley Luty, a nineteen-year-old single mother, disappears from the Llanerch Diner parking lot on August 23, 1982. She is five-foot-two and a hundred-and-ten pounds. A man with a thick square mustache leaves the diner just before she does and speaks to her outside. The report is sure to mention her history of epilepsy and that she parked on a dimly lit street across from the diner, indirectly blaming her for her own absence. The man mentioned is listed as a potential witness despite his immediacy in her final known moments, never a suspect. She drives away in a green Chevy Impala borrowed from her stepfather and vanishes into the night somewhere in Upper Darby, Pennsylvania. She is reported missing by her stepfather. Both she and the car are still missing.

Confession: I am a shameless paranoiac. I instinctively believe every lone male in parking garages, grocery stores, crowded mall, and otherwise public space is following me. I tuck my purse under my jacket and shrink myself to inhabit as little space as I can. I carry keys between my fingers on the walk back to the car. I check every window before bed. These precautions come from my father, who through some unfortunate circumstance believes girls like me are fated for violence someday. He's seen something – many things, as the stories accumulate over the years – and he sees me. The world has too many moving pieces that can snap me like a twig in a cogwheel. The world is out to get me. I must survive in a world where I am prey. I'm here, fearful and feminine, and I look just like Shelley Luty.

***

"You have such a good body," Mom says to me while we're shopping for a prom dress. "Why don't you show it off more?"

I'm in floor-length black gown with cinched sides and a plunging neckline. A clip holds the excess fabric tightly to my back. I rub the arch of my foot on the edge of the carpeted pedestal, my hands curling and pressing against my defined thighs. My waist dips inward, partially due to the uneven tilt scoliosis bends in my hips. Extra breast cups to fill in the dress lie scattered on the floor after some trial and error.

"No, too young." The tailor says from the hem of my dress. Her stringy hair tickles my hand when her bun bobs up to retrieve another needle. "Too young for black too. Black for ladies and widows. You are still girl."

"She can wear whatever she wants," Mom says from behind me. She smooths my hair with her fingers, bending and twisting a wad into a mock updo. "I think she looks classy."

Classy, another word for acceptable – modest, refined, but with a hint of sensual potential. It falls on the scale somewhere evenly between whorish and prudish, naked and nun. Mom and I exchange grimaces towards the bright tulle and rhinestone skirts stuffed in metal racks like sheared lion manes; we slide slick comments to each other about the kinds of girls who keep their curls unpicked after the iron shapes them into stiff coils. Everything not classy is trashy. We're not nice but we keep that to ourselves. Classy is the highest compliment I could hope to receive, but I watch myself move in the mirror and I am too much. Too eye-catching. Too visible.

"No, too sexy," the tailor says. "She will be woman forever. Girl, only once."

Confession: my clothing choice is deliberately designed to negate all attention. I have a waist Mom envies, breasts a size unfittingly large for my short thin frame, and long legs that I could flash if I ever needed to call a taxi in a bad movie. I'm pretty by standards set forth by my mother and aggressive old men at the grocery store. The vagina seems to be the ultimate treasure, the holy grail searched for by violent men with a statement to make. I bury myself in my clothes to make myself smaller, smaller, smaller. I have the privilege of intentional dress, intentional shrinkage, to hope I am ignored and someone else

157

is followed. Survival is a cruel game of shifting spotlight, hoping the fixture breaks and crashes onto anyone but me. I am the most selfish person I know.

***

I only speak to my paternal grandfather for two obligatory minutes at a wedding. I know three things about the man: he is my father's father, his agreed upon name is Pop-Pop, and my distance from him is calculated and intentional. I remember nothing about him personally, and without the dusty photograph buried in a cedar chest in the living room, I would believe I never met him at all. But I'm there, six or seven years old, in a room with white tablecloths and dark wood ushered forth by familial expectation and my nervous father's hands. Pop-Pop is in a wheelchair. He might have glasses, be bald, call me something like sweetheart or darling. For the brief public moment, I pretend I've been his doting grandchild forever, and he my proud grandfather. Neither of us mentioned the distance between us, the awkward spaces and familial eyes boring into our skins. Somebody knows something, but nobody bothers to speak up about it for years.

Confession: I missed his funeral. My parents didn't want me to hear something I didn't know. There's a lot I still don't know and will never know, and maybe I'm connecting threads that aren't there, but these moments revolve around a singular paradox of comfort and anxiety. I'm afraid to ask about my grandfather. Rumors go that he was an in-between man for the Philadelphia Irish Mob and the local branch of the Teamsters Union, a coalition of truckers known for a shady underbelly. My parents would tell me stories later, tidbits of history otherwise buried in the ground with him, and the reason my hands sweat when I think about going in public alone starts to come together.

***

We're talking about ghosts the first time I hear about Shelley. The house is dark except for the weak table lamp and quiet for the electronic drone of some television show on in the background. I'm sitting in the living room, on top of the couch with my legs swung over the back. Dad is in the kitchen, offering me various alcohols in the fridge because I'm home for the first time since turning twenty-one. Mom stands by the back door, cigarette smoke twirling towards the moths crowding the porch light.

"That wasn't a ghost," I insist. "That was me being a creepy anxious kid!"

"It was not you," Mom says, "you were asleep when I checked on you. How could it have been you?"

"I know it was me because I remember it," I explain and gesture towards the landing on the staircase. "I stood in the corner because I was afraid to tell you guys that I was scared, so I just stared at you until I went back to bed."

"I don't know about that," Dad pipes up, "but I remember a little girl at the side of my bed that wasn't you."

"I didn't know you believe in ghosts too," I say.

"I don't know, but I've seen some stuff I can't explain."

"Like?" I lean forward, excited to indulge in the hidden spiritual history of my father. I nearly knock myself off the couch, tipping it slightly before throwing my weight back to stabilize it again. He shifts and crosses his arms, looking to Mom who urges him on with the wave of her cigarette.

My father drops a bomb on me. He says, like it's nothing, "I saw my stepsister Shelley once after she disappeared."

"Your stepsister disappeared? When was this?" I was stunned.

"1982," he continues softly. "I was nine years old."

His father had left his mother and remarried a woman with daughters, and they lived in a house in Upper Darby before moving to New Jersey. He often slept on the couch due to some familial complications I never got a straight answer about, and though he might not have been nine in this memory, I like to imagine a skinny boy with ratty bedhead curled up in the couch cushions staring at a ghost.

Shelley walked through the living room, a cloud of teased brown hair in true eighties style. He was brief about his memory, but he described her distinct and underwhelming height, thin frame, everything the police report notes even now. She had a scar on her arm shaped vaguely like a tree or a triangle; I found the same recount of a scar that shape and size in her description on a missing women's website.

"It was Shelley," he says. "No doubt about it."

"What happened to her?"

"No one knows," Mom says and flicks her cigarette. "But if he saw her ghost, you know what that means."

"Why didn't you tell me?"

Dad pipes up and turns away to grab a beer. "The rumor is that my Dad had something to do with it. He was into some shady shit and it might've gotten Shelley stuck in the middle of it. Also—don't go researching her after this. You'll just end up upset."

People don't just disappear. They have physical bodies, remnants of existence somewhere in the world. Something happened to her. My grandfather's involvement in the Teamsters' dangerous games might have made him a target for backlash. At least that's my theory, and if it should prove true, that would explain why a stepchild in her stepfather's car – a car marked because of its owner – might disappear. I know now why Dad wanted me to avoid researching Shelley because it has divulged one realization that I've denied myself until now: I'm angry.

If Shelley had a purse with metal edges like my father advised, would the man she'd spoken to in the parking lot have left her alone? If she had worn something over her waitress uniform like I craved to in the dressing room, would she have caught his attention? If she hadn't borrowed her stepfather's car, a beacon of revenge on a mean old man with a green Impala and a pretty stepdaughter, would she have arrived home safe to her two-year-old? The possibilities enrage me. Even if she had those things, taken those obsessive precautions I've so desperately adhered to, would she have even been a single percentage safer? How small must we be to be invisible? I'm older now than Shelley was, even smaller, even lighter. How easy would it be for someone to grab hold of me on my walk to the car? How easy would it be to disappear?

Confession: I want to crush throats with my hands. I want to bend thumbs, break arms, bite through skin and taste blood in my pretty mouth. I want to wield my own protection without guilt. What's riskier: being seen or being invisible? I sit in my house with the itching paranoia that at any moment, the discovery of a young woman home alone could spell death should someone decide I am their victim of choice. I periodically take precautionary laps around the ground floor, reviewing the locks on the windows and fantasizing about escape routes until someone comes home. I want to be so violent and aggressive that everyone is afraid to mess with me, but in practice I'm soft, small, invisible. What do you do when you live in the contradictory state of safety? What's there left to do but wait until someone chooses you for prey and you have one moment to decide whether you will be endangered, or dangerous?

- Leah Skay

Cluck

Police have pulled me over twice this week about my orchids. They think I can't see the road through the forest on the dashboard and the trellises over the back windows and the pots hanging from the wing mirrors. I say jungle predators have the best eyesight on the planet. They say not on the bypass to Grinshill.

Both times I'm let off because Mr Car smells so much of fertiliser and my laundry and sleeping bag. And I keep the windows up because chids need body heat, especially in winters like this. All the same, once a week I roll one down outside Maud's new semi-detached.

On the freezing lawn, my son Jeffrey guides ants into a more efficient path. He recoils a bit when he sees me, but not much.

"Hey buddy!"

His back says no thanks. Not a talker, our Jeff, but Maud says he's treated well at the new school, has laminated his timetable and stuck it on his bedroom wall, with annotations.

Steve's marching out in his bathrobe. "What do you think you're doing?"

"Nothing! It's me, Steve. Jason." My hands have gone up.

"I know it's you. Stop harassing my boy."

I can't tell if he's joking. "He's my son, Steve, come on." Obviously he knows that's my son.

Two 14-year-olds crash outside, hoofing a ball: Steve's sons from wife number one. The ball whacks Mr Car. "Careful!" yells Steve, forearm on my roof. Jim and Marcus pound upstreet, laughing.

"Just like my Jim and Marcus," I say, pointing out Orchid Jim and Orchid Marcus, hardy twin dendrobiums. Steve pats my roof.

Now Maud appears in the coat I bought her in Aberystwyth. My heart goes watermelon — Maud could shave her head and wear a binbag and still no one would believe she married me.

"Here's your sustenance." Maud scowls. But a wonderful smell escapes the tupperware she hands through the window.

Steve rocks Mr Car until curry slops onto my lap.

"Steve, come on! There's Jeffrey's inheritance in here," I protest.

That's a fact. Splicing Jim and Marcus has produced a breed native only to the glovebox of Mr Car. There's no research to oppose it; Orchid Jeffrey must be worth a fortune.

"Just jokes." Steve lets go and spanks the boot. "Enjoy your free meals."

Mr Car stalls first time, as per tradition. Maud puts a grin into Steve's back. Steve puts his foot on the bumper and Mr Car lurches off like a supply teacher with his shoes tied together.

In the overhead mirror, Jeffrey catches my eye, looks at the dirt.

***

The best nutrients for orchids can be bought online for scary money or gathered for free from ordinary chickens. I drive 40 miles to a stretch of the Severn where a battery farm ejects waste into the river and crack my window to let in the fumes — only a smidge. It's the coldest night of the year and brown ice nudges the banks.

I will sleep here tonight.

Later, almost midnight, the motion-activated lights of the compound blaze. I wake up and scan the riverbank, thinking: am I in trouble? Then I see—

Oh my god. Jesus Christ.

Oh my god oh my god oh my god. Where's my scarf? Jesus, oh my god.

"Catch it! Catch the end!"

Oh my god oh my god please.

Hrrrgh.

Oh my god Jesus.

Hrrrrgh.

Oh my god Jesus he's so cold. He should be shivering. God what do I do. Push his chest. Hand over hand. Ha ha ha ha staying alive. The whole song or just the chorus? Please god, I only know the chorus.

With a spasm, the young man barfs himself alive. He lies back and pulls the scarf that saved him tightly over his eyes.

***

I pile Jim and Marcus on the backseat, Maud and Steve on top of them, then the young man into Mr Car and set off for the hospital, at which point he rouses, pulls out a drowned lighter and starts flicking.

"Hey, come on," I say, "the fertiliser in here is very flammable."

He tosses out a drowned pack of cigarettes. "Buggered anyway."

Then he stares away at the hedges, curled under the seatbelt like a blanket.

After a while he mutters, "I only meant to scare them."

"What's that?"

"I didn't think the whole house would go up. He should've kept away.

I told him, my sister isn't made for his harem. And now my life's over, because he wouldn't keep away, now I'm dead and where's my 72 virgins, because he wouldn't keep away?" He coughs. "Stinks in here."

"Sorry. It's the fertiliser."

He begins to notice - and be impressed by - the sheer volume of plant-life inside the vehicle. "You a druggie?"

"Far from it," I laugh. "The one you're squashing is Mrs Hayes, my old Geography teacher. By your elbow is Megan, my aunt who slipped me a fiver every Christmas. I keep them going and they keep me going. It makes you glad to live when you matter to this bunch, believe me."

"That works?"

"Of course it works. Why even ask that? Of course it works. I'm not the unhappy one."

Too much. He flings off his seatbelt. "Stop the car."

"I don't think I'm allowed."

"Stop the car or I'll rip these plants up."

I pull over on the scrap of hard verge. Around us, fields deepen their sea-floor hush, moonlight stands crisp in the air.

He curses. "The handle's covered in something."

Yes, fertiliser. I get out with bad grace and walk around the back of Mr Car. It wobbles as he shifts seats. Then Mr Car makes a grinding sound and rampages off down the lane.

"Hey! Come on!"

I stagger to a halt, watching the headlights define the 40-mile maze of hedges into town. In seconds, a fly-style buzz, then nothing.

Coldest night of the year. My chids are gone and I'm left in a t-shirt.

Just like that.

I want to cry.

***

My name is Hugh and a hilarious thing about me is: I'm alive. I'm on fake time and everything's funny.

Do I feel bad? Of course — more gunge for the guilt pit. But I have a positive plan about that, which is: Drive to the sea, hide on a ship, goodbye fucking Hugh. The plants love it, cheering every pothole. He was right about them, endorphins in the spores.

Then I think: The Syeds' house is news by now. Footage of me on social media. My sister. But if I'm gone, she's safe.

So cheers the happy green crowd: Go faster while you're still free!

***

Coldest night of the year, no phone and no shelter, I, Jason, am up turd creek. Homeless folks die on nights like this.

Is this it? Is this how I go?

Would anyone care?

Shut up. Two Jeffreys depend on me. Nonetheless it's 40 miles back to town, no way I'd last the trek, plus why would he stop there? He might sell Mr Car to be compacted in a strange town, Jeffrey's first buds crushed...

Sobbing! Sobbing now!

Shut up. By the river there were lights meaning warmth. I cut through fields, shortening the distance. Lot of gleaming eyes in this one. The next one, all dark. I stub my knee on a watering trough, thinking: something drinks here. Yup, I hear thunder. I'm over the hedge, minus one trouser-leg, when the bull crunches the gate like celery.

After two miles I'm numb, shuddering with cold; then I smell ammonia. I glimpse the battery farm by moonlight, circle it twice, shout and wave and cause the floodlights to come on. I even shake the fence but nothing comes out except more wind.

I think: Something exits.

I fight the wind to the riverbank and look down. There's the pipe. Wide enough, and no grate.

I look back at the compound: About 40 metres.

40 metres of unthinkable hell. Otherwise, death by exposure.

I suddenly recall Jeffrey's sweet head back when it bobbed, too young to support itself. This here is in no manual, but this is when it counts. I squirm into the slimy reeking darkness of the pipe.

I never ever wish to talk about the pipe.

A heavy grate admits me to a darkness wonderfully warm. I strip off my slime-chilled clothes, hearing sleepy warbles echo like prayers in a cathedral.

I stand in a bleak channel between cliffs of cages, each holding a dim sort of lump whose feathers spill down like snow.

Something furry brushes my calf.

All through the pipe I felt followed but that was paranoia. Oh Christ, it wasn't. That's a fox, zooming up the cagefronts into the gloom.

Trespassing's bad enough, but letting a fox into a henhouse means jailtime even if you were extremely cold when it happened. So up I go; the cagefronts make easy but painful toeholds. Before I rest and consider how to rescue Mr Car and Orchid Jeff, I might as well catch a fox with my bare hands. A rattle eight feet above, a rebounding cage door... I reach it and insert my head and, yes, there's a fox inside, hissing because the cage is empty.

Yes! And then:

Not good.

I can't remove my head. It went in like nothing, now my ears are trapped. The fox hisses and claws my nose; I scrabble, kicking lower cages and triggering a gothic choir of panic. Cornered and now deafened, the fox mauls my face in earnest; I scream, causing chicken bedlam. The fox resumes the onslaught till I scream again, this time because my toes have slipped and I'm hanging by the ears. The fox cringes back from the noise.

Up close, its snout is crossed with deep scars. In its eyes is a frank, unhappy need which reminds me of someone I never think about, or try every minute not to.

***

From her loose hair and raw skin I suspected she might have wanted free drugs/compensation. Nurses were trained to look out for it. Her symptoms were unprovable; I gave her an embellished prescription and, feeling good, moved on. An hour later I was called to the head doctor's office to answer the allegation that I had performed a rectal exam for my own perverse gratification. "Are you sure?" he asked three times. Of course sure. I was extremely married to the eighth wonder of the world.

It spiralled; a cloud of suspicion turned to thunder; whispers became torrential. In the canteen, colleagues edged away or fled. Still, nothing came, no follow-up, no baseless inquiry. It didn't matter. I was sweating through my scrubs by day and hearing voices next to Maud at night. When at last I surrendered my employment, everyone - including those who showed furtive sympathy - was grateful.

Go on, piece the rest together. Maud left, took Jeff, remarried in less than a year. I kept my chids and Mr Car, my last friend.

I confess all this and more to the fox, who scrabbles at my face when I fall silent. I tell him/her about my son Jeffrey, bright as Einstein, about Maud and Steve, tight as two peas, about Orchid Jeffrey whose rareness guarantees a big return. And the more I talk, the hotter my eyes get, the stiffer my throat, because I never talk about myself, not ever, and what I'm hearing is news from outer space. Things aren't going well. I'm not happy any of the time. This isn't something I can write off as funny: homeless, naked, head stuck in a cage, facing feral claws. And I'm fighting, I realise, every day, fighting just to stay afloat, or a punchline — why? What universe reserves this situation for you and cares if you keep fighting?

For the first time in a long time, I make a decision about me: No more. This is where it stops. This is the lowest I can go.

***

Whoever you are, wherever you find yourself, whatever you've lost, know this: Morning comes.

Two guys with torches find me dangling eight feet up, nude and ranting about forgiveness. They have questions. Once reassured that my intentions are normal (ie not here to shag the livestock) they manage to free me with soap. The fox is then captured with a handheld trap like a big webbed pair of tongs and presumably set free.

I reveal the big truth distilled from my night of hell: "I need to find my car and see my son."

"Dressed like that?" says the moustached one.

So I pull on my cold, sopping clothes. Moustache agrees to drive me towards town (where he has an errand) and drop me near the rag-and-bone yard to start looking for Mr Car.

Hope's pilot-light burns gradually through the mist around the van. Fields rear like wings in the slow updraft of light as all becomes dawn.

"Can't see a damn thing," Moustache moans, projecting his ire at me through the windscreen.

"Would be good if we were panthers," I say, seeking common ground. "Jungle predators have the best eyesight on the planet."

"That's eagles," he snaps.

Well, not a biggie. Still got hope.

Around a bend, tyretracks crush a five-foot hedge and slew towards a misty oak. Against the oak, a blackened, crumpled car lies smoking.

"Stop, please, that's him! In that field."

I hare through the ridged earth towards the oak. Mr Car's airbags have turned to ash and the chassis is a cartoon concertina. A skeleton sits charred at the wheel, hands stuck to former rubber. Squares of plastic are all that's left of my beloveds.

I reach through the smashed window and open the glovebox. Orchid Jeffrey's stem is in bits, miraculously green. Dead without knowing it…

The pilot-light gutters. You try, don't you, you try and try but you're always worth a good kick because there is no bottom to it, how much you can take. It's always a joke: that's your role.

"Don't cry, man," says Moustache. "I'm calling the police. Just wait and we'll see you right, okay?"

I dry my eyes because my arm can still move up to my face and dry them.

"I'm going to see my son," I tell him. "Don't bother. I can walk from here."

…Into the low sun for nine miles, through hedges and hoarfrost and spider-hung lace, past barns and broke-backed cottages, through to neighbourhoods with garden furniture and Christmas lights. Maud's new semi-detached has robins on the roof: bright jittery apples. I'm going to see my son.

"What happened to your face?" Maud asks on the porch.

"A fox bit it."

"A fox bit your face? One fox?"

Steve jogs downstairs in his bathrobe.

"It was a fox," Maud says, pointing.

"Try to shag it?" Steve jokes.

Maud asks, "What happened to your clothes?"

I take a deep breath and come clean. "Orchid Jeffrey is dead. All of Jeffrey's inheritance is gone. I effed up."

Steve sighs and grips my shoulder fondly. "Well no one gave a crap, so that's fine."

I begin to thaw. It's fine.

"I'm going to see my son," I say, and brace myself to come to terms with why I can't.

Maud and Steve share a mild shrug. "If you want a shower, right is hot, left is cold," says Maud.

***

Jeff is in his room, walls neatly tessellated with maps and diagrams and, bizarrely, the station timetable of Gare du Nord. I loom awkwardly, keeping my toes between the lines in the carpet.

"Hey buddy. It's me, Jason. The fact is I'm your father, like it or not, and I haven't been a role model, I hope I haven't, but I love you and you should have a better life than me because my life is rubbish and I love you so much." Jeff doesn't turn from his MacBook Pro. Defeated, I sit on his bed.

"What are you working on?"

He says, "The cross country tournament is biassed against Year 8 who race first after lunch. But my model accounts for relative rates of digestion."

What a kid. I don't deserve him. But I know now to try.

"Could your model apply to the cultivation of new orchid seeds?" I ask.

"I think so," says Jeff, after thinking. "But the model is based on numerical metrics, so I'd need that. And you probably need to drive off."

There's no criticism in his voice but my heart picks up its own dagger, taking aim.

"No more," I tell my son. "I've got nowhere else to be."

- Matt Ingoldby

167

Little Wind

We begin with the still-beating heart of a dove,
which sounds much like rapturous applause.

We come to a pane of glass pitted by moonbeams;
as if starlight muted through a pitcher of cream.

In the meantime something like wind blowing out
of a desert canyon is blowing from out of a desert canyon.

If you'll turn to your left you'll find the world turning to the right.
You're approaching the centre; we are always coming to the centre.
Always we are coming to a precipitous edge –
a slippery acre, tacky with both ecstasy and dread.

Next, a chapter some will find indigestible.
You've been under the constant influence of its shining mountain,
one emotion wearing the coat of another emotion,
a little wind whispering *spiritus spiritus* . . .
Let's call this a well, shall we, or a quilt of crimsony gravitas.
It puts me in mind of arms crossed over the chest of Pharaoh.
Which is like sunlight eating away at a stone.
Which is what lives under the pebbles on the planet Mercury.

Behind us, a ravenous mouth of one some would call Death.
Below, a wheel composed of pollen and shame.
Over our heads, the air temperature falling.
But it's what lies ahead that must most concern us;
an amorphous thundercloud composed of colour and light.

This may be a thought reflecting on a mirror.
This could possibly be a memory forgetting itself.
Or it might be nothing more than a dream turning over in bed,
its heart still beating, its eyes mad-red, its message incomprehensible.

- Bruce McRae

One Night In Ten

It was the eleventh day of Christmas.
I awoke to the sound of pins marching.
The dark was raining its felt hats.

I rose several times, uninventing the bed.
All through the house I felt it,
the presence of another, of another's hands
making little tea cakes from dreamy remnants.

I walked among a surplus of darkness,
room to room, floating several inches in the air.
Mice were stirring their cauldron of heads.
I sensed the unliving conferring with roaches.
The neighbours' dreams were playing loudly next door.
Peeking past a curtain, I saw the stars scratching.
I thought of frozen cubicles, cubes of blue ice,
a thousand innermost thinkings.

The moon had been replaced by an errant cloud,
by a streetlight on the fritz down the road.
In the wooden houses I could hear ears listening
to the long scraping of year into year.
A summer's day flashed its breasts in my mind.
Perhaps I was dreaming, like a fish, with my eyes open;
that I was sleeping like a horse, standing up.

This revelry was broken by a crack in the pillow.
A voice called to me. Like a flower opening.
Like a door pushed shut by the passing wind.

I drifted days, or seconds, on the sea of my breaths.
I returned to the scene of my accidental birthing.
The bed whirled in tempests of quietude.
Many times I lay down before closing my eyes,
my mind's eyes, which went everywhere
and saw nothing.

- Bruce McRae

A Little Chat With Ourself

I'm talking to you through a rip in the seaside,
out of a warmed dent in the passing nothingness,
from behind a loop of tightly woven angel-hair.

I'm talking to you, and the wind is rubbing a cornfield.
I'm telling you the sun is sawing its right hand.
That the moon is a knothole in God's coffin,
the stars His marred and excitable match-heads.

I'm going along, caught between a feather and a flower.
I'm shouting from the top of my voice,
from the foot of the stairs.
I'm talking to you from a squeak at the circus.
Pointing out opossum's breath.
Explaining, carefully, gunpowder.

I'm telling you the world is a fog of consciousness.
I'm telling you about the mountain chain
that's fallen in love with a river.
About a river pouring itself into your tea.
About a cup of tea embarrassed by the cosmos's antics.

You're listening to me spouting forth
from the swirling vortex in mommy's sewing machine.
You've been asleep under a stone for a thousand years.
You're hearing my voice, but believe it's the rain falling,
and that each cold drop is a planet or miniature Himalayas.

I'm talking to you from the ragged hum of my hands.
I want you to realize that I'm snow
drifting in a far-off land.
I want you to see how the world still loves you.
To know the stars understand.

- *Bruce McRae*

Disappearing Act

It was the only disappearing act I could do,
when I was flattened up against
the yellow papered kitchen wall, almost losing my
balance when my heels tried to move
further back than the thin molding,
as my father leaned over, so his face
was nearly touching mine,
red and purple with rage,
eyes bulging, bloodshot,
words and spit flying out of his mouth
as his pointer finger repeatedly jabbed me in the chest,
hard enough to make sure I would feel it the next day;
when he gently shook me awake,
wrapped his bear sized arms around me
so tight I lost my breath.
I held on, mute,
safe in this moment alone.

After he had gone upstairs
I tiptoed to the kitchen for breakfast,
and tried not to spill the milk.
I sat to eat my cereal,
unaware I did not reach the edges of myself,
but quietly peered out,
from some dark place beneath my skin.

- Karlie Powers

171

Personalization

A woman walked past me. She was wearing perfume, I happened to notice even though my sense of smell isn't as powerful as a dog's. She was wearing a lot of perfume—or the perfume was strong regardless of quantity. I suspected both factors were at play—she'd sprayed a lot of perfume on herself, and the perfume was strong. The scent was nice. It was sweet. I recoiled, nonetheless. I was embarrassed for her, maybe. It was obvious she was wearing perfume. It wasn't subtle. I'm conditioned to believe tend the use of cosmetics and fragrances ought to be subtle. I may be wrong. Anyway, she approached the pickup area and waited. I was sitting at a table, drinking a cup of coffee. There was no milk or sugar in my cup of coffee. Plain is good enough for me. I fancy myself a simple person. I wasn't privy to the details of her order, which she'd placed via an app on her phone. I suspected it wasn't simple, though. I suspected it involved modifications to the default options, a substitution of one ingredient for another and no this and an extra that. She didn't fancy herself a simple person. I envied her a little. She was more honest, maybe. More open, more transparent. I wasn't wearing cologne. I was wearing deodorant. I'd purchased a stick of deodorant at the pharmacy, not long ago. I'd stood in the aisle and struggled to decide among the varieties. Classic. Fresh. Musk. Unscented. I chose one of the scented varieties, ultimately. My vanity was exposed. This isn't a story about me, though. It's a story about the woman who'd walked past me and attracted my attention. A barista was preparing the woman's latte or macchiato, adding a drizzle of syrup or whatever. She glanced in my direction, once or twice—unless it was my imagination, unless she was glancing at something behind me or to the left or right of me. At any rate, I didn't gather the impression she was in a hurry -- until her name was announced, at which point she kicked into gear. She hurried past me, trying to move swiftly without spilling her beverage or tripping and falling. She was wearing high heels, which increased the level of difficulty. I marveled at the woman's confidence and comportment — inwardly, though. I didn't turn around and watch as she exited the store and ventured into the parking lot. I didn't betray any interest in the spectacle of her.

- Peter Reibling

By the Time I Made Oklahoma

I didn't learn to drive until I was nineteen, and a sophomore in college.

It was Spring Quarter. I needed one more credit hour to round out my full-time schedule, and Driver's Ed fit the bill perfectly. One hour per week, for ten consecutive weeks, of combined in-class instruction and in-car training in a specially-purposed, automatic VW Lady Bug. Having grown up in Vietnam where the main choices of city transportation were the family bicycle or a three-wheeled jitney cab, or in case one was privileged enough to be able to afford it, a moped, I wasn't as caught up in the automobile culture as American teenagers typically are. In my naïve young mind, driving was more of a future necessity—for when I officially joined the workforce after graduation in two years' time—than an imperative rite of passage.

That's not to say I was impervious to the thrill of ensconcing myself behind the wheel and taking control—or at least attempting to—of the wonder machine for the first time in my life. In fact, it gave me a rush like no other, an exhilarating sense of power and freedom, that concrete feeling of being master of my own destiny. Like most young people before me or since, I took to it like a duck to water, just out of sheer enthusiasm, such that after merely seven in-car sessions with the instructor, one every week for half an hour, I managed to pass the driver's test (parallel parking included) and proudly posed for my official DMV license picture.

For the next two years, however, I never had another opportunity to slide into the driver's seat of a car and take the wheel again. And thus by the time I graduated and accepted a job offer in Pittsburgh, Pennsylvania, the sum total of my driving experience still consisted only of those scant hours in Driver's Ed around the small Ohio college town where I went to school. In other words: totally inadequate.

Having been informed that I would be doing a fair amount of business traveling in my new job, one of the first things I did after arriving in Pittsburgh was to hire an instructor to give me a refresher driving course. Two or three evenings a week that summer, at the end of my workday, he would come pick me up at the downtown hotel where I was staying temporarily and take me to go practice in the hilly neighborhoods of the city. Besides brushing up on the basic skills that had gone rusty over years of unuse, I also learned to drive in city traffic and on hills and slopes.

It was a good thing I hadn't waited to do that, for my first test came sooner than expected, when a senior colleague and I were called into the boss's office one morning.

"You guys are going to Texas next Monday," he announced. Then, turning to me, "You've mentioned you'd like to get involved with the new project at our plant in Wichita Falls, right?"

I nodded eagerly, and the boss continued, "So John will accompany you down there and introduce you to the local staff. Then he'll take off, but you can stay another couple days to get acquainted with the team and discuss the project. How does that sound?"

I thought that sounded fantastic: at last, a major project to sink my teeth in and prove I was cut out for the job. But I didn't realize then just how big a moment that actually was, which only became clear when John and I got together later to work out the logistics of the trip.

John was a senior engineer in our recently formed group, about ten years older than us kids that had been hired fresh out of college. Smart and experienced, but more importantly, funny as all get-out and one of the nicest people around, he was a great role model as well as a mentor to all the junior engineers. We would run to him with questions and for all kinds of advice, which he was always generous with, no matter what the subject.

"So," John said to me, "we'll rent a car at the airport and drive to the plant. And since I'm leaving the next day and you're staying, we should put the car under your name so you can keep it for the duration. You okay with that?"

"No problem at all," I answered quickly while doing my best to calm the butterflies in my stomach. "I've got a current driver's license."

A car all to myself. For three full days, perhaps even longer. In wide-open cowboy country, no less. It certainly felt like a momentous event in my budding driving career—a challenge I had been priming myself to meet head-on. What made it even more special was the fact it was taking place on my first official business trip, as part of my learning on the job.

The following Monday we landed in Wichita Falls in the late after-noon. The secretary had called ahead and reserved a midsize car under my name, so all I needed to do was show up at the rental counter inside the airport, present my driver's license, sign the prepared paperwork—and out the door we strode, with key in hand, into the parking lot.

"It's just about dinner time, so let's go check in at the hotel, then we can grab a quick bite and unwind afterward," John suggested. "You drive. I'll navigate."

Crouching behind the wheel of the rental car, which seemed like a boat to me (it was true what was said about the sizes of things in Texas, I not-ed), as I tried to exit the unfamiliar airport I was suddenly seized with hesita-tion, even with John sitting by my side. As I crawled to a rolling stop before an intersection with no traffic lights, craning my neck every which way, I heard him say in his calm, helpful way, "You can pull up a little further, you know, *and then* come to a full stop. It'll be easier to see."

Merging onto the highway was another matter, a bit of a tense exer-cise since I hadn't had much practice doing it and there seemed to be a ton of truck traffic barreling by at top speeds at that hour. I managed to squeeze on but remained safely in the right lane, often hugging the thin white line on the shoulder's edge to stay clear of the powerful wake from eighteen wheelers in the outside lane.

"Whew," I said, gripping the steering wheel tightly with both hands while training my eyes on the endless blacktop ahead. "They drive *fast* down here, don't they? Or am I going too slow?"

"You're doing fine," said John breezily. "There's plenty of room on the road for everyone. Those truckers are actually excellent drivers. They'll get around you if they have to."

Reassured by my mentor's unflinching support, I settled down and followed his direction to the roadside hotel without a hitch. We promptly checked into two adjacent rooms off the parking lot then headed out to dinner at a nearby Texas Barbeque joint, another first for me. Upon return, as I looked up at the sunset still lingering in the summer sky, an idea struck me.

"There's still daylight left," I said just as we reached the rooms. "I think I'll take the car out for a little drive around the block. Get more comfortable with it, you know?"

John paused for just a moment before proceeding to unlock his room's door.

"Hmm . . . all right then," he finally said, turning to me. "I'm just going to watch some TV then hit the sack. You drive carefully, and don't stay out too late. We have a full day tomorrow."

Before John had disappeared into his room, I was already in the car, mapping out a plan of action. It looked like there might still be a half-hour of daylight, plenty of time for a spin around the block, and then a quick hop onto the highway, up to the next exit and back. A nice, easy run. I should be able to make it back before dark, no problem.

It was awesome driving a car by myself for the first time, without an instructor or someone next to me navigating—and coaching. I felt like a bird, free to explore anywhere I wanted with no constraints or pressure, spurred on by seemingly unlimited power at the tips of my toes.

The area surrounding the hotel appeared to be sparsely populated, which in fact made it an ideal practice course. I zipped around it a few times, delighting in how smoothly the car glided, how light and easy the power steering felt—how quietly the engine purred. Upon completing the last go-round, I hung a turn and entered the on-ramp. Pressing steadily down on the gas pedal, I sensed the engine revving before it kicked into high gear, and a big smile broke out on my face as the vehicle shot onto the highway.

Traffic had thinned out by this time, and the merge was much easier and smoother. I rolled down the windows and let the warm evening wind rush through my hair—a sensational feeling I had never before relaxed enough to notice or enjoy as a driver. It was such a thrill to just fly down the flat open road with no destination in mind that I decided to skip the next exit and drive on a while longer.

Soon, however, as the final daylight began to fade, I reluctantly told myself it was time to head back. The next off-ramp took me through a convoluted loop under the highway, to a four-way stop. Disoriented and unable to make out the signs in semi-darkness, I opted for the easiest choice and hung a right, in hopes that would lead me to the on-ramp in the hotel's direction. To my dismay, the ramp was nowhere to be found—only rows after rows of poorly lit warehouses. Panic ensued as I tried to backtrack by making a series of turns and circling the blocks, which only seemed to lead me farther astray. In the process, I even drifted down the wrong way on a one-way street, causing an oncoming motorist to lay on the horn as he swerved wildly to avoid hitting my car head-on. This moment of white-knuckle terror left me breathless and shaken.

After wandering, lost and confused, around the maze of dark buildings for what seemed an eternity, I was more shocked than relieved to emerge back on the main street near the exit where I had come in earlier. More incredibly, I found myself on the proper side of the street this time, because looming ahead, on the overpass, was the highway. With immense relief, I spotted a sign for the elusive on-ramp and quickly followed it onto the big road—beyond anxious to rush back to the safety and comfort of my hotel room.

It was nighttime now, and the unintended detour had left me drained. The combined effect made it difficult to notice the road scene around me, until a large sign hanging from an overpass caused my head to snap up in attention. I blinked twice before doing a double take. Announced in big letters on the well-lit sign was the name of the upcoming destination: Lawton, Oklahoma.

Oklahoma! Speechless, I let out a soft whistle. How in the world?

Earlier on, in my excitement and great hurry to get back on the highway, I must have taken the wrong on-ramp, heading north instead of south. Wichita Falls, I had heard, was very close to the state line. How close? I hadn't expected to find out the answer quite this way.

Fortunately, the first exit after the sign happened to be a gas-and-food stop, with a lone gas station next to a roadside restaurant. Both places appeared deserted, but together they formed the only island of light in the vast darkness. Having learned my lesson, I decided to leave nothing to chance and to stop and ask for directions this time. I pulled into the station, parked, then traipsed into the small office–convenience store. The young attendant hopped off his stool.

"Howdy," he drawled, no doubt welcoming a break in the doldrums. "How can I help you?"

I ran my fingers through my hair. "Where am I? How far is it to Wichita Falls?"

"Uh-huh," he said with a flicker of mixed curiosity and amusement in his eyes, "you're in Oklahoma, just inside the state line. Wichita Falls is fifteen miles south of here. When you leave, turn left on the road out in front, then you'll be crossing under the highway. The on-ramp is on your left. Can't miss it." Saluting with a finger to his forehead, he added, "Good luck, sir."

I thanked the attendant, crawled back in the car, and proceeded as directed. With no further complications—thank goodness—I arrived back at the hotel fifteen minutes later, and a couple of hours after I'd left it. Pulling into the empty space in front of my room, I put the car in park with the engine still idling and slumped back in the seat, my head knocking against the headrest. As I was rubbing my bleary eyes and slowly catching my breath, I heard a door yank open.

John stepped out of his room next door, a dark silhouette against the lighted background.

I straightened up and shut off the engine before scrambling out of the car.

Hi there," John said with admirable composure. "You're back. Everything okay?"

I gave him a sheepish smile. "All good. You're still up."

"Oh, yeah," he said, shrugging. "I saw the headlights in the window and thought it might be the police bringing you back."

Before I could explain or apologize, he waved me off. "Goodnight. Let's get some rest and be ready for tomorrow." With that, he turned and slipped back in his room, as I watched the door close behind him and the light go out.

The next morning, on our way to the plant, I gave John an abbreviated version of my late-evening adventures. He chuckled good-naturedly and cracked a few jokes, essentially brushing the whole episode off as no big deal and already in the rearview mirror. His assurances calmed my jitters and took a huge load off my mind just in time for our meeting.

At the end of the day, however, as he was getting ready to leave for the airport, John drew me aside and made sure, "You all right by yourself here for the next couple days?"

"I'll be fine," I said with a confident smile and my head held high, before hurrying to add, "I just won't go driving around after dark."

I kept my promise and made it safely back to General Office in Pittsburgh a few days later. John was the first to greet me, with a cheerful "You survived. In one piece!" All my fellow new hires within earshot cocked their heads up in obvious curiosity. Smelling trouble, I slunk into my office just as John, raconteur extraordinaire that he was, began to regale his fans with the zany details of our night in Wichita Falls. Giggles and laughter streamed into my office for some time, and I resigned myself to the reality that I had now become the latest chapter in the office lore.

Moments later, I was typing up my trip report when I heard a soft knock on the door. John poked his head in, a big smile on his face. "You realize, don't you," he said with a wink, "we're not laughing at you. We're laughing with you."

There wasn't much I could say or do in response except to bare my teeth—as in grin and bear it. For all the worries and concerns I had caused the man, payback was only appropriate.

In retrospect, this innocuous anecdote about my first rental car on our first business trip together added a colorful dimension that helped cement the mentor–mentee bond between John and me. Such supportive friendships, in those early days when I first joined the American workforce, were what gave me the confidence I needed in order to assimilate and grow. They made my first job a rewarding and memorable learning experience.

Years later, after having lost touch with each other following job changes and relocations, I stumbled across John's contact information by chance, and we reconnected. On our first phone chat in decades, the mere mention of "that time when I crossed the state line into Oklahoma . . ." worked like a magic mantra that instantly opened the floodgates of memories and laughter.

"You know, John," I said in between chortles, "I still can't get over how you kept such a cool head that night despite everything happening. You were amazing and I really appreciated it. I knew things could have gone totally sideways and landed us both in a world of trouble."

He cracked up. "Why do you figure I couldn't go to sleep until after you got back? And then I kept wondering on the flight back the next day, will the kid live now that I've left him there all by himself with the freaking car?"

The truth, they say, always comes out in the end—even if it may take a few decades.

- C L Hoang

Refuge

And I sank into the soft muck of myself,
cool and damp, when I didn't know
what to say, where to place my hands,
how to stand up for myself. And it was fine
in the dim light by the rock wall I'd erected.
I could play with spiney arthropods,
gather and arrange the pastel shells
of mollusks like a prayer circle around me.
I could dream of female breath, just that one
who would appear one day out of nowhere
and understand everything about me.

In the salt-soaked mud I was everything
I could imagine, beyond insult or bullying.
I was brother to a chain of lovers, sisters
of the sea who lifted me on ivory shoulders,
one or the other of them waking me in my real bed
from another perfect dream. Clasping my hand
in a moment of mutual sympathy for our lost mother.
Both of us knowing the day would come
when nothing out there would stop me.

- Alfred Fournier

179

The Urban Gardener Who the Bulbuls Hate

There is no doubt that Dashrath the temporary gardener who comes to tend to the unruly plants on our coastal balcony in Bombay is a man on a mission who dons his city-bred persona every time he shears the crowd of palms and flora in the guise of pruning supported and patronized by my well turned-out wife even while the gruffy mountaineer in me laments this hacking every three months but Dashrath hadn't appeared with his giant shears for some time because of the lockdown and so I reveled in this highly busy little balcony garden with the sea breeze whipping the foliage even while this pair of freaky shrieking jumpy bulbuls did their sprightly dance every day at dawn in what my wife called 'these overgrown bushes' which I hold dear full with the knowledge that the two little bulbuls who pretend to be adults come here only because the 'bushes' are 'overgrown' and when the birds jump from twig to twig and branch to branch it is a sign that the bulbuls and I are on one side and Dashrath and my wife are on another where the former uses his shears like she uses her tweezers to sternly excise nature of all kinds to meet the demands of the city but this time when Dashrath comes after two years of a lockdown and after my miraculous return from a Covid ICU with the bulbuls and the overgrown plants telling me that life is beautiful and definitely worth living I stare at his shears with much concern and my wife with a feeling of normalcy sparkling on her brightened face and when Dashrath declares war on the plants the bulbuls scream and jump off to a neighbor's balcony.

- Ash Kaul

What Made Him Eat

To get him to eat, his father told him he was a cowboy once
and the cattle he herded later became steak,
their usual Sunday dinner, and the story would repeat
along with the value of potatoes, and for that,
there was the famine, and because his mother was short
and he needed to be tall like a man, he would eat the meat,
and the French meat pie on Monday,
the peas and tuna on mashed for Tuesday,
spaghetti and fries on Wednesday,
meat loaf with ketchup on Thursday
 and finally frozen fish sticks,
on it would go, until needing more meat,
cube steak replaced the pasta, the grey vein-pounded
beef, pan-fried, hot water added for gravy,
that he would chew into a veined ball of grizzle and spit,
and feed all he could to his dog until once when caught,
his father said that feeding meat to the dog,
to this stray found two winters ago,
its long mongrel body rib defined, bone-poking even,
would turn him wild, and that all dogs turned wild
and if fed meat long enough, would rip out your throat
to eat meat again. That night before bed, the boy
laid out a rope of clothesline almost the length of his bed,
slipped a noose knot over the dog and turned off the light.

- Michael Foran

Aunt Margie's magic book

is two hundred years old, mom tells me.
A grimoire full of potions and spells
handwritten on yellowed brittle pages,
notes in the margins, chemical stains

and dust, brown dust, probably
old blood. Your aunt always hid
her fire-maimed hand—a concoction
went bad, a missing ingredient.

Tried to bring back what couldn't be
all because the damn recipe called
for a bug which is extinct.
Love is like that, mom says

it's magical, then poof, gone, and no
matter the page, something will always
be missing, save the best alchemy
for yourself.

- Richard Matta

The Outside is Endless
-for Tomas Transtromer

Spring 2015 and Transtromer has sprung
His ragged Winter claws and burrowed away

The Aurora Borealis is in mourning and Sweden Hangs down sad-long against
the Season's

Anti-Gravity while a people
Sit with grief and grief's refractory

Outline of a ghost as geographic shadowbox
The ocean's purse gray and digging

At a nation's head where this time of the year
Tumescent Spring shoots pink

And green by yellow and by purple too
Mirroring the great ravine of space

The Poet dreams of returning in the form
Of a glacier calling fjord in the sun

Warm and cold and strong for their newfound
Selves running motionless for the coast

And the God of the clouds cries out of the clouds
Faith is absence

The poets are first in line for reassignment
And in the Next I am continuously alone

- Paul Koniecki

Born Blue

The old man arrived at the pavilion one Sunday morning saying he was there to work. He wore ragged rust-colored shorts and a field hand's floppy black hat. His eyes sagged like open sores, and Angeline wondered, vaguely, if he was sick or drunk, or something even worse.

You have a swimming hole to run, he said, sweeping the air with his wooden oar. Concessions to sell. You need me to keep out the wastrels.

He told her it was his calling, boatman, and that he'd come to keep her property clean of cheats and deadbeats and idlers.

She looked at him, raggedy old man that he was, and sighed a sigh of defeat. Her swimming hole, as he called it, was a quarry on the outskirts of town. A broad blue lake in a granite bowl, fed by a cold clear spring. It was so deep, the kids who swam there said it had no bottom, and every year, as if to prove their point, one of them went looking for it, and drowned.

The price to get in was 50¢, and they came all summer, from all around the county, to swim and carry on and do what teenagers do in untamed places. She and Robert would watch them make out under their beach towels. Young dreamy-eyed boys finger fucking their girlfriends, their wanting-to-please girlfriends giving back in kind with deep kisses and languorous handjobs. The jukebox played the summer's Top Forty all afternoon under lazy blue skies, and the sweet scent of suntan lotion lingered in the air like a seductive perfume.

Angeline believed it was the easy nature of the place that dared them to take chances. With no rules to abide, and no one to watch after their doings, they had no reason to put a rein on their desires. No reason to look aside from temptation.

They're kids, Robert would remind her. Same as we were. They're young and wild, and long as they pay their way and don't cause me no trouble, I leave em alone.

Over the decades, some struck their head on rocks, diving. Others took cramps and floundered. A few simply disappeared beneath the surface of the lake, no one ever knowing the hows or whys of their pitiful ends. The water claimed them equally and without conscience, boy and girl alike—the tragic, the wild, the just plain foolish, who, as Robert said, were victims of their own stupidity and nothing more. He called it "nature thinning the herd."

Folks drown, he said in his flat deep voice. They drown in rivers and oceans and even bathtubs, and there's nothin you or water-walkin Jesus can do about it, honey. It's just the way things are.

The drownings were the cost of doing business, Robert insisted whenever Angeline raised the matter. It was the price you paid for the bottomless thrills of playing in a rock quarry. This swimming hole of theirs, he told her, meant as much to their livelihood as the family farm. They depended on the money it brought. The bills it paid. With all deference to God's loving bounty, he told her, it was the quarry, not grace, that put food on their table.

Robert had grown up with the quarry. So it struck Angeline as odd he had never learned to swim, and even more odd that he had never wanted their daughter Jenny to learn. But he had his reasons. He said if you can't swim, no one can ever blame you for not jumping in the water. I've seen it when people drown, he told Angeline. Their first thought is to take somebody down with em.

Angeline remembered the day the Sheriff's deputies came with their rowboats and grappling hooks. She and Robert were only just married, and she'd never seen an operation like that before, solemn men in sweat-stained khaki uniforms slinging iron barbs across the water as if they were fishing. A boy had struck his head while roughhousing with other boys, and disappeared in plain sight. They'd searched for him, but without luck. So the lawmen came and cleared the lake of all the swimmers, and spent the afternoon dredging the water.

I can't swim myself, Robert told one of the deputies, otherwise I'd have gone in after him.

Angeline walked up to the farmhouse alone that afternoon. She left Robert to close the concessions stand and lock the gates to the ticket booth. She couldn't look at him after what she'd seen and heard. Couldn't stomach the thought of seeing his cowardly face at the dinner table. They slept in different beds that night. But the following morning Robert rousted her and led her by the hand down to the pavilion.

It was a sunny morning. Not a cloud to be seen. The gates wouldn't open for another hour, but a line of swimmers was already waiting at the ticket booth. See there, Angeline? He pointed. Life goes on. Not because it has to, but because it wants to. I know you're shook up right now, but you'll get over it. You'll see.

***

"I don't need no boatman," she told the old man, pointing to the sign over the pavilion's iron gates: SWIM AT YOUR OWN RISK.

But the boatman persisted.

She said, "Water don't have no conscience, old man, and neither do I. You swim here in my quarry, only person you got to answer to is yourself."

"I'm a boatman," the raggedy old man said, from under the shadow of his hat brim. "I'm not here to judge. I'm just here to keep out the ones that don't belong."

She crossed her arms.

"You've got a swimming hole to look after," he said again. "You can't keep up with this place alone."

Her brows rose, slightly. She wondered if he'd heard gossip about Robert's accident from one of her neighbors down the road. The quarry was all Robert left her when he died, besides Jenny and the house. The farm had gone to his brothers. The insurance money to his ex-wife, Darla. And yes, the old man was right, she couldn't keep up. She'd fallen more behind every summer. The boatman propped himself on his oar as she considered his offer. She looked to the trees on the far shore, and bit the inside of her cheek. All she ever wanted out of this life was what she had coming. What was owed her. But all life ever did was take from her, and keep on taking.

The place was losing money with Robert gone, and the losses got worse every summer. Jenny was a well-meaning child, a good daughter and a good worker. But she was hardly her father's equal when it came to manual labor. They struggled without having a man around. That was the truth of it. And the boatman was right, the cheats and stragglers would ruin her if she didn't do something soon.

She looked him up and down, weighing her options.

The broad brim of his black hat shaded his irascible, sunburned face. "I'll take five dollars a day to patrol the water," he said. "Four, if you let me sleep in the boathouse."

She could hear Robert's muffled groans all the way from the cemetery up on the hilltop. Five dollars a day! But Robert was gone, dead in the ground from his own stupidity, and she was still here, breaking her back, doing all the work with no help from anyone.

She unfolded her arms. Laid her hands on her hips, and nodded, reluctantly. "All right," she said to the boatman. "You got yourself a deal. Take your possibles down to the boathouse. You start this afternoon."

***

Some summers earlier, long before the accident that took his life, Robert nailed a sign over the entrance to the pavilion. It was arched, painted like a rainbow, either end of its brightly colored bands resting on a plinth of clouds.

The words on the sign read: THROUGH THESE GATES PASS THE MOST BEAUTIFUL GIRLS IN THE WORLD.

Their daughter, Jenny, was one of those girls—a blue-eyed beauty, lithe, and long-limbed—flawless but for the withered arm she'd carried with her since birth. Jenny was almost seventeen now, bravely naïve, and to Angeline's great disappointment, ripe for seduction.

The boy who would come to steal her innocence was from a broken home. He lived with his father, who was rich, and like his father he was used to taking what he pleased, believing whatever he saw, and wanted, was deserved if not owed him.

"Do you know that boy?" Angeline asked one of the girls who'd strolled up to the concessions stand the day he'd first appeared. She pointed past the girl's shoulder to the tall blonde figure standing on the rock ledge on the other side of the lake.

The girl turned and peered over the top of her sunglasses. "I wish."

Angeline frowned.

The second girl in line, the one standing behind the wishful one, was older and more sensible. She flicked back her long dark hair and said, "I know him. He goes to East High."

The girl told Angeline the boy's father drove a red convertible and wore a thin, gold mustache. Gold rings on each of his fingers. He owned a used car dealership, the girl said, and she'd heard from her mother's best friend that he drank like a stevedore and threw away women like they were empty bottles.

***

Jenny was standing in the shade beside the picnic tables when the golden-haired boy first appeared. She was joking with a group of kids who had just come up from the beach with towels around their shoulders. She was writing down their lunch orders on her small green pad, and he stepped out into the sunshine—bare-chested and bronzed, like a water god—and the smile on her face went slack. Her arms slipped to her sides.

The boatman, who was patrolling the far side of the lake, rowed up under the rock ledge and threatened the handsome young thief with his oar. But the boy laughed, and shook back his long blonde locks and danced a sailor's hornpipe as the old man teetered on the boat's thwarts, swinging the wooden blade.

Angeline's eyes narrowed, catlike and suspicious. The handsome blonde thief had cheated her of her fifty cents, but it wasn't the lost money that troubled her when she watched him dive over the boatman's head into the water. What troubled her was the silly, love-struck look on her daughter's face as the boy resurfaced, laughing, taunting the old man.

***

The boy came every day after that. He was broad shouldered, a strong swimmer, and he would steal down through the trees and dive into the water and swim circles around the boatman's skiff, agitating the raggedy old man until his sun-scorched eyes burned feverish under the brim of his hat.

187

Crowds of rowdy boys and girls would gather on the shore to shout and cheer their skirmishing. But Jenny would watch from a distance, careful not to smile or applaud the boy's antics. She would, on occasion, rise on the balls of her feet and bounce nervously if the oar swept too closely to the boy's handsome blonde head. But otherwise, she kept her feelings locked away, deep, deep in her heart, which only sharpened Angeline's concerns.

One day the boy swam out to the plank deck in the middle of the lake and strutted among the sunbathers on their towels, beckoning Jenny to join him. Again the boatman gave chase. But again, the boy proved too clever. He taunted the old man, then dove into the water only to reappear on the other side of the skiff and backstroke his way to safety.

Angeline had hoped that Jenny's deformity would deter the boy. Her withered arm had proved a glorious impediment to such entanglements in years past. But her body had come to ripeness under the sun that summer, and the light in her pretty blue eyes welcomed his advances. When the boy appeared, she would hook her clawed hand behind her back in coquettish in-nocence, allowing her long legs and shapely bottom to convince the young swindler there were other, more enticing interests worth his consideration. It was easy to look past the withered arm, Angeline discovered, if your interests, like the boy's, lingered elsewhere. It was easy to see what you wanted to see, and believe what you wanted to believe.

What's wrong with you?" she longed to say to Jenny. "Can't you see what he wants? Can't you see he's gonna break your heart?

But she kept her silence.

The nights were long that summer, and she would lie awake in bed in fear of being left alone for the rest of her life; nothing to her name but the quar-ry. She would whisper into Robert's pillow, pleading for advice, saying How do I talk to her? only to have her words die in the dark like the unanswered prayers of an orphan.

She hated Robert for dying. But even if he were alive, what could she possibly expect from him? He was a farm boy, coarse and uneducated. He'd died a simpleton's death, suffocating in a silo accident. Drowning in a downpour of grain without ever knowing the first thing about love or loyalty or betrayal.

***

One evening as she was drifting off to sleep, Angeline heard a car rumble up the gravel road toward the farmhouse with its radio playing. It stopped at the edge of the wood some distance away, and the headlamps went dark. After a moment, the music stopped too.

She slipped out of bed and went to the window, but there was nothing

188

to see. A little while later she heard what she thought were voices, though she couldn't be certain because they were drifting in from so far away.

A little before dawn, restless and still unable to sleep, she tiptoed down the hall and stood before Jenny's door. "Honey?" She pressed her ear to the wood. "Jenny, honey?"

No one answered, so she rapped lightly and turned the brass knob. The door creaked and a breeze blew through the tall curtained windows. The sheer drapes billowed, drifting over the wooden floor, but the girl's bed was empty.

***

There were boys who would sometimes swim out to the float deck cradling heavy stones in their arms and leap feet first into the water, betting they could touch bottom. Some would last longer than others. But in the end, they all met with defeat. Their friends would lean over the planks and peer into the water, counting out the seconds, while their girlfriends looked on with frightened expressions until, despoiled of their heroic notions, they burst up through the surface, empty handed, lungs sucking at the sky.

Angeline thought about these boys as she lay in bed that night. Their single-mindedness. The way they risked their lives for what they couldn't touch, refusing to believe that some things were, and always would be, beyond their reach.

At breakfast the following morning, she did her best to stay away from what her heart wanted her to say. Instead, she asked Jenny how she'd slept. "I thought I heard you fussin in the middle of the night," she said, gilding the lie with an innocent smile. "Or maybe I was just imaginin it."

Jenny, who was staring idly at the poached egg on her plate, came round at her mother's words, and casually picked up her fork. "You had a bad dream, Momma. That's all." Her eyes were red and puffy, and so were her lips. But she smiled when Angeline reached across the table and touched her wrist.

"Are you all right, honey?"

"I'm fine, Momma."

Angeline looked at her daughter's beautiful young face, and remembered the long night of her birth. How she came to them breech, her tiny arm wrapped around her neck. Her skin a tepid shade of blue.

The midwife had bathed the baby and swaddled her in blankets, assuring Robert and Angeline she would be fine after a few days. Time, the midwife said, would make everything better. She advised Robert and Angeline to rub the arm, frequently and vigorously, saying it would help the flow of blood to the muscles, and they did as she said only to be told later, by a doctor, that the therapy had permanently damaged the nerve.

Robert refused to accept the diagnosis. Determined to undo the harm

189

he and Angeline brought down on the child, he bound Jenny's good arm to her side to force the withered limb to function. But the experiment proved fruitless. As would others. Finally he built a body-stretching machine from old harness straps and bits of iron that had grown cobwebs in the barn. It was a horrible, demeaning contraption, which in some ways made it seem appropriate to the task. But in the end, it too failed.

Angeline was not mechanically minded like Robert. But she, too, was convinced the deformity could be diminished. If it couldn't be rectified by means of medicine or machinery, she told herself, it could always be disguised. So she had Robert refurbish the old treadle sewing machine in the attic, and went to work. She ordered bolts of cloth from a catalogue, cut patterns from butcher paper, and in a few months time managed what neither the midwife's therapy nor her husband's barbaric carpentry had been able to accomplish. She tailored an entire wardrobe of dresses and blouses with fitted sleeves that hid the deformity, leaving Jenny as normal-looking as any other little girl.

She ran her finger over Jenny's wrist now, stopping when she saw the bruise on her daughter's arm.

Without thinking, she pressed her thumb to it.

"Ouch!" Jenny said, jerking the arm away. "Why did you do that, Momma?"

Angeline had no answer.

Jenny drew her arm to her side, and went back to her poached egg, while Angeline turned and stared out the window.

The frown on the girl's brow lingered a moment as her pretty blue eyes sorted their way back to the secret place she'd been dreaming of before her mother had bothered her. But Angeline wasn't finished.

"He's bullyin you," she said, moving away from the window.

Jenny looked over, sharply. "What?"

Angeline glanced away again, embarrassed. But then she glanced back, eyes hardening. She had admonished herself not to say those words when she sat down to breakfast this morning. Yet they came out anyway, on their own. They didn't have to, but they wanted to, and her heart gave voice to them before she could find a way to stop her tongue.

"What are you talkin about, Momma?"

"I'm talkin about that boy," Angeline said. "That blonde-headed boy. He's bullyin you, and I don't like it."

Jenny laid her fork on her plate, rose from her chair and looked down, pitilessly, at her mother. Clearing the table in silence, she stacked the dirty dishes in the sink, then turned and went upstairs to dress.

***

When she returned to the kitchen, she was wearing her swimsuit. "You don't know anything, Momma," she said, brusquely. She was clutching one of Robert's old tee-shirts, and she tugged it over her head, down her shoulders and over her breasts. "He loves me," she said, "and I love him."

Angeline wondered how much of that soft young body her daughter had already given to the golden haired swindler. What sort of down payment she'd made hoping to keep him by her side. She shook her head. My God, but she was a silly stupid girl. Did she truly believe one arm would be enough to hold a treasure like him forever?

She wheeled on Jenny. "What's wrong with you?" She didn't mean to cause more trouble, but she wasn't able to keep the question to herself any longer. "Can't you see what he's doin, honey? Can't you see what he wants?"

The girl stiffened, clenching her teeth. "What's wrong with me?" She laughed, bitterly, thrusting out her withered arm. "This is what's wrong with me, Momma! This is what's wrong!"

Angeline's eyes brimmed. She felt herself drowning. "Does he have a name?"

"Yes, Momma," the girl said, coldly. "He has a name." But she didn't say what the name was. Nor would she. Because she knew without knowing that everything she kept from her mother, she kept for herself.

"You've always been a perfect daughter," Angeline said in a voice near to begging. "Your father—he wanted you to have a good life. An easy life. So do I." She turned up her eyes, pleading. She wouldn't admit she was alone in the world without Jenny, but the truth was there in her face for anyone to see. "Please, honey. Don't."

"Don't what?"

"Don't sell yourself short."

The girl straightened and gave with a crooked smile. "Sell myself? Short?" Her lip curled into a sneer. "Have you seen him, Momma? He's the one who's perfect, not me."

***

When evening came, Angeline left a note for the boatman after closing the gates to the pavilion. She slipped it in an envelope, and tacked it to the boathouse door. The envelope contained a week's wages, along with a twenty-dollar bill marked with a red X.

In the note, she told the boatman, Do whatever you need to keep that blonde-haired boy out of my quarry. See that he never swims here again.

She walked up to the farmhouse alone that evening, the same way she'd done all those years ago when she'd heard Robert spew his lies to that deputy. She wouldn't have any more deceit around here. She wouldn't have any more swindling. She wouldn't allow the quarry to take anymore from her than it already had. There had to be an end to things, and this was it.

That night she dreamed again about the boys who swam out to the float deck cradling stones in their arms. Their reckless desire to have what could never be theirs, groping after what they didn't deserve. Believing they could have it if they just held their breath long enough.

She woke late the next morning and dressed and went downstairs, relieved to have put such a bothersome night's sleep behind her. But when she walked into the kitchen and saw that Jenny had already eaten and gone down to the pavilion, her troubled mind returned. She thought about the note she'd left for the boatman. The twenty-dollar bribe she'd slipped into his pay envelope. She worried Jenny might see the envelope tacked to the boathouse door and know what she'd done.

She turned on the teakettle and dropped a slice of bread in the toaster. She thought about the boatman and the boy...the bruise on Jenny's arm... about how Robert died in that grain silo, leaving her with nothing in the world but this cursed swimming hole and no way to manage it.

The screen door clattered shut behind her when she hurried out of the kitchen. The toaster popped and the teakettle whistled.

She ran all the way down the gravel road to the boathouse, but when she arrived at the pavilion, she found the gates open and the ticket booth empty. Swimmers were milling around under Robert's rainbow arch as if it were a holiday. A crowd had gathered on the beach, and there was some sort of commotion taking place on the far side of the lake.

She raised herself on her tiptoes but was too short to fetch a glimpse of what everyone else was seeing. So she pushed her way through the throng until she reached the beachfront, panting and out of breath.

She looked across the water. There, near the rock ledge on the far shore, she saw the boatman leaning over the side of the skiff, his floppy black hat riding low on his eyes, his wooden oar in one hand, the blonde boy's long thick locks twisted in the other.

"Look," someone gasped. "He's bleeding!"

It was true. A bright red rivulet oozed from a cut on the boy's forehead. But he was alive and fighting, and in no danger of drowning.

The sudden shock of blood had drawn their attention away from the girl on the other side of the lake who'd leapt in to save the boy. She was flailing, fighting to keep her head above water, but her face was already blue.

- *Robert McGuill*

192

Hair

Washed clean as snow in the original epic. Plaited first in Africa. Egyptian women buried with extra braids. Flowed from Spartans on the field. Used in sacrifice. Beeswax to hold styles in place. Wigs made from the hair of slaves. Fishbones of the first comb. Mullet, crimp, perm, Jheri curl. An envelope of baby hair. Cleopatra and Marie Antoinette known for. Cynthia Antoinette your name. Your brush of captured sun. Your scrunchie alive in old light. Hair you fought and tamed and sometimes hated that I inherited, had done weekly if you could, how it's hard to say if it's anywhere in the ash, fine as dust or pollen, but without the heat or the blaze of the gold that made it so.

- Jen McClanaghan

The Chase

The sun drives the seasons; these were the dog days between Legion ball and football practice. On one of those warm Friday afternoons, I turned my Harley onto Diagonal Boulevard.

These were the best of times—running with Richie and his brother Larry, living on unemployment, sponging off the old man—more interested in getting laid than getting paid. Traffic tickets, pecker tracks in the back seat, a police escort home after midnight. Mom pacing, wringing her hands like Lady Macbeth, crying out loud, "Where did I go wrong?"

A mile from home, the bubble machine lit up on a cop car parked at a side street. I grabbed a handful of throttle—my risk insurance had expired; that meant no license!

The Harley roar and the siren alerted mom on my way past the house, wind in my face, the fuzz on my ass. I looped on 74th Street and flew past Marlys Pederson's, my fantasy until Phoebe Crouch ruined me on the first day of seventh grade.

At Portland, a busy thoroughfare, I said a prayer, goosed it and blew across without looking. I opened my eyes and was surprised to find myself alive with a good lead. I glanced over my shoulder. The cop stopped to look both ways. Once he crossed, he saw my left onto Stevens Avenue. Cousin Buzz leapt up from the dinner table and ran into the street when he heard me shoot past.

A block from a quick exit to Bloomington, the next jurisdiction, I forgot that Stevens ended in a tee. I swung my wheel hard left into a lowslider, wiping out against a chain link fence. I abandoned the bike and sprinted barefoot into the new subdivision.

It was time for the empire to strike back. Patrolman Starcevic slammed on the brakes and took off after me on foot, followed by the intrepid Buzz who had a special low regard for Starcevic, and was quite upset that the cop had his hand on his gun the whole time. More cops arrived. My flight ended when I found no cover, gods, or friends in the featureless backyards. Surrounded and captured, yes, but Buzz didn't give up my name; he called dad. The cops perp-walked me back to a cruiser and loaded the fallen bike into a trailer. The only thing missing was the Marine Color Guard.

The Richfield police station was a modest affair in those days. The cuffs came off. They sat me down in a bust chair and questioned me at a beat-up metal table in a small, grimy-paneled room. When my inquisitors were satisfied with getting nowhere, they cuffed me again and took me downtown to an impressive stone fortress, the Minneapolis Courthouse.

I was booked by the Minneapolis cops. They rolled prints, took pictures and escorted me into a steel Vatican. Clang! Every door that opened revealed more doors and more rooms, until I lost track of whom or where I was. When the last door slammed shut, I was alone in an old fashioned cell like in the Westerns, except without the flies or Gabby Hayes. I was claustrophobic and panicky. I understood why people commit suicide in their cells; all I could do was meditate on my self-inflicted wounds and captive state.

It wasn't General Lasalle who rescued me from the pit and the pendulum, just dad. He bailed me out before I had time to entertain or befuddle my jailers. At home, I ate the supper that mom had saved for me and opened the mail. Oh, Mr. Postman—there were two days remaining on my insurance—I had been legit all the time!

Life goes on; sometimes we have no choice. The next day, Richie was plying his girlfriend with roses, trying to get in her pants; her cousin was on her back in a flashy dress, legs up, chewing gum, smelling pretty. Forty-eight hours later I knew why—*Pedpiculosis pubis* and *Neisseria gonorrhoeae.*

Richie talked to Larry who was positive I would only get six months in the workhouse. That was the very thing I wished to avoid. I decided to plea bargain and called the Richfield City Manager at his home. He found an army recruiter who agreed to take the morning off and go to bat for me. (God bless him or the money that changed hands.) The trial took place in a room noted for its shabbiness. Mom and the recruiter sat together. When my case came up, the audience tittered as the clerk read my rap sheet, and then went into hysterics as he ticked off the new charges. What a gas.

The recruiter stood straight. He made a rousing speech—honest, I had no idea who he was talking about. I got a fine and an invitation to join the Army that day, instead of the joint. Perfect timing and sound geopolitics—the Berlin Crises was over and Vietnam hadn't ramped.

Children, ask not what your country can do for you, ask what you can do for your army recruiter.

Au revoir, idiot.

- Charles Jacobson

Oil and Nectar

Soft roses and gasolines drippings in dipped eyeliner passings
Drift by a swift reply you've marked me in dust
Paintings you promised so long
Wrong it was to pray to a saint

- Ashley Schmidt

What If the Roses Don't Smell?

You promised me they would.
Made me believe that I had done
Something beautiful.

They're not.

Instead, I have this garden I never wanted and didn't cultivate
And you, stomping all over it in your rage to get me to admit
I am what you tell me I am.

I'm not.

I don't even like roses. They're too cliché.
Too delicate.
They have thorns like looking in a mirror.

I can't smell the roses
They have nothing to offer me
I can't smell the roses
And it's killing me inside.
Wake up and

What if the roses don't smell?

- Eva Nemirovsky

Certain Silence

I used to know a guy who liked to commit petty larceny up by the college. He'd steal bikes, maybe, or grab loose change and like half-eaten packs of M&M's from cupholders, and this guy, Doug, he was a real wizard with locks. Quick fingers. He once lifted the AmEx straight from my wallet just to prove he could do it, and I almost ratted him out after that kid disappeared. Gave the cops his name and address as like, you know, an anonymous tip or whatever. Not that I thought he had anything to do with it. It was more like guilt. Like not wanting to wake up in ten years and wonder what if, and I do sometimes. Wonder. I think about how I saw him at that ballfield over on Laterno right around that time, and everyone felt the anxiety floating around, the pressure, even though it was like no one dared mention. College kids going missing near interstates. Bodies of water. Doug had a cigarette in his mouth and a softball bat in his hand, and I walked up there. Dusk. Indian summer or what have you.

"Looking good," I said.

"Short on cash."

"Like always."

"Was thinking of heading up to campus for the old glove box shuffle, but all that shit going on up there, you know. Might be bad timing."

"They'll think you're some kind of perv," I said.

The cigarette fell from his mouth. Doug had these fucking reflexes, man. Quick flick of the wrists and the bat was on it. You could see embers like wet fireworks, weakly groping through the air.

"Wouldn't be far from the truth," he said.

There were two cop cars in the parking lot, and we laughed. Put up our hands and waved at nothing, at shadows or ghosts or lampposts. I thought about guns and rivers. Mosquitoes hung around near Doug's face, and I wondered if you could ever solve crimes via insect, and yeah, I thought. Gotta be. This day and age. There's probably a million ways to collect all our little floating droplets of blood.

- Brett Biebel

198

The Lesson

Have you ever wanted something so badly
        your body would surrender its skeleton,
               its tendon and ligament,
                    to make space for the want?

Something about the thunder
        of today's happenings undoes
               me like the closet's orphaned skein of yarn.

I miss my family, my state
        of mind, the nakedness of my native

California. I long
        for days at the lake where
               my white back charred like a bell pepper
                    one summer with my cousins, for the island
where a couple buddies and I
        canoed with a pod of dolphins:
                    their sleek, gray bodies
like polished sportscars, for the redwood forests run
        through by rivers and highways

with such ease it almost makes me weep.

I miss the mountains, rough
                 like a lover, miss
the meadow where breathing
        wildflowers and elk once felt like heaven,
                    innocence, existence.

It was here my father taught me to follow him
        through the brutal night.

I believed climbing
        Mt. Whitney—a day of starvation and altitude
               sickness—would bond us

because I thought love meant suffering,
                  meant hating

oneself to make room for the other.

- Christian Paulisich

199

-Al Dente

Will it always be like this,
this odd awkwardness?
We've fought again
and it wasn't the ex you still texted
or the dinner you didn't
invite me to, it was the television.
I asked you to press play
and all our prickly parts broke loose,

shredding our loveseat.
Each time I think
I'm getting good at this dating thing,
another misunderstanding
brings us to our knees. Words fail me.
Before, I thought love was everything,
all-engulfing, easy
yet impossible.

I find myself in the kitchen, again,
swearing this is the last time,
knowing it isn't.
I want to make
you love me.

Watching the Food Network
when I was younger, Giada
said to toss the pasta into the sauce
with ease, *facilmente*—
what I imagined love
to sound like—she said to listen
to the pasta talk to you. And I do.
And I do. And I do.

- Christian Paulisich

Secondary

Born from the bare walls of that dark room
that would only ever have one occupant,

you somehow grew faster than my firstborn, you
who never fussed, never punctuated the small

hours of morning with a wail or stood
beside my bed at 3am waiting. You were not

a finicky eater, not one to give up naps early or start
walking late. You've never had much in common

with your brother. Under other circumstances you
might have been a smile in a picture frame, another

load of laundry, round two of algebra homework.
There were years when I thought you were playing

hide and seek, and looking would be enough. I never
found you. You never revealed your hiding spot.

Maybe you forgot how the game worked. Maybe I
was playing it wrong all along. Now you are

the thinnest sliver of imagination. Now I can
hold babies again. I'm finally the age

when no one asks after you anymore.

- Merie Kirby

[One year in every ten/I manage it—]

—a line from Plath's poem, Lady Lazarus

The insect on the roof of your mouth buzzes and flutters. He tastes like salt, and then bleach. The plastic bands hugging your wrists cut into your skin. Someone is asking your age. Is this your wrist/Is the nurse still there, smiling/ frowning, pushing your tongue away? The sheets make you colder, so they give you more sheets, bury your face in icy angles.

Three hummingbirds sip from the angle of your elbow, they pinch and swear. Pink warmth blossoms from their bite marks. The side of your neck itches and stings. More men line up near your feet and ask you to look at their fingers. Why is the alarm calling your name. Who are these mourners, lined up and stripping your chest? For hours your face stiffens, as if holding a grin.

- Christine Hamm

Doll Parts

We come sleeping with our eyes open. We come sealed in fragile cellophane, heated and molded in China. We come through the mail, through the mall. We come with raw edges along the crown, the chin, to catch and bite.

We come with open palms – we come to hold anything you tell us to hold. Our fingers sprout stubby and identical, rubbery on girls' tongues and teeth, easy to swallow and swallow again. We come naked or with painted dresses.

We come with club feet, small lines painted where the toes should go; we come with white plastic slippers like little listing boats, easy to lose and tear. We come tame, we come satiated, full.

We come with stout legs that do not bend. With glowing pink/orange skin. With a lingering chemical scent that makes girls drool. With a cloth torso covered with prickly cheap cotton. With no marks for nipples, no space for a cunt.

We come with painted eyelashes and enormous, widely placed eyes. With dry eyes. With Betty Boop eyes. With pupils easily scratched off with a fork or fingernail. With colorless lips that always pout, but never open.

We come with ears too small for our heads. We come ready to lay forever in an abandoned suitcase, slowly flattening face first; ready to sit in the corner of a trunk tucked into a moldering house, infested dresses scattered under bed springs, burst jars of canned peaches flooding the pantry. We come to those eager to break, to burn.

- Christine Hamm

Art Imitating Life

It's that moment. You know the one. When a new art exhibition is about the be revealed. The hush that falls over the once chattering crowd. The shared anticipation for experiencing something for the first time. Knowing this is the last moment the world will exist without this masterpiece.

Our artist, Nolo, seems cool and collected. You wonder if he's really that way, or if he's masking his bundle of nerves. He's done these so many times, it should be as common as putting on his shoes in the morning. Not that he ever wears shoes. Or wakes before noon.

The gallery's curator, Michelle, is beaming with pride. Or is she just thrilled about how much money she's going to make. Nolo has made her rich. And will continue to do so. She gives him total freedom in his creativity. It always pays off.

She has made her speech and moves to unveil the exhibition. Here is that moment. One that is so rare, but so beautiful.

The curtain is pulled away with a flourish. You cheer and clap along with the rest of the room. The enthusiasm is palpable. You're so excited about what is revealed you're not actually seeing it.

The applause quickly tapers off. There's a sense of confusion. A hint of disgust.

The hush turns to quiet mumbling. Then anger.

Michelle cautions us to remain calm. Digest before we judge. But her voice is as shaky as yours would be if you had to speak at this moment.

What you see is indigestible. You want to vomit. Like Nolo has just regurgitated all over the art world. Over human decency.

Art must be raw and disturbing. That's Nolo's motto.

But this is a shit show.

Nolo's latest exhibition is a recreation of a school shooting. Spread out on the floor before you are bodies of dead children. Pooled in blood.

Simulated.

You hope.

Something about this feels real. Too real. Emotions flood you. Disgust. Pain. Sorrow. And yet, a nervous giggle burrows up from your lungs.

You want to look away, yet your eyes are drawn to the details. Blood and bullet holes cover the walls. So many bullet holes it's ridiculous.

You find yourself thinking of the many bullets that fly in these situations. And you wonder why the hell there would ever be a situation like this. Never mind more than one.

I'm holding a mirror up to society. Is that what Nolo said?

If the world saw the pictures of these horrible events, people would be called to action.

But you signed all the on-line petitions. You posted all those articles on social media. What color ribbon was school shootings?

We need to shock people into waking up. Nolo contends.

You agree. Art should disturb. And this does. But why should you be its target? Address those who can make a difference, like lawmakers and gun manufacturers. Present this at an NRA convention.

All you want to do is get away from this room. Drown out these images with mindless entertainment. Drink, smoke pot, sniff coke. Numb yourself. But all you can do is stare at this horror disguised as art. And wonder. What more could you do?

- Thomas Misuraca

Contributors

Millicent Borges Accardi, a Portuguese-American writer, is the author of four poetry collections. Her awards include fellowships from the National Endowment for the Arts, Fulbright, CantoMundo, California Arts Council, Foundation for Contemporary Arts (Covid grant). Yaddo, Fundação Luso-Americana (Portugal), and the Barbara Deming Foundation, "Money for Women."

Devon Balwit walks in all weather. Her most recent collections are *Rubbing Shoulders with the Greats* [Seven Kitchens Press 2020] and *Dog-Walking in the Shadow of Pyongyang* [Nixes Mate Books, 2021].

Kaitlyn Bancroft is a reporter with KSL.com in Salt Lake City, Utah. Previously, she's written for *The Salt Lake Tribune, The Spectrum & Daily News* (part of the USA TODAY NETWORK), *The Denver Post, Deseret News,* and *The Davis Clipper.* Follow her work on Twitter @katbancroft or on Instagram @katbancroftreports.

Christopher S. Bell is a writer and musician. His work has recently appeared in Alluvian, *The Bookends Review, Saw Palm*, and *Quibble*. His latest novel, *Contemporary Disregard,* will see release by year's end. He currently resides in Pittsburgh, Pennsylvania.

Brett Biebel is the author of *48 Blitz* (Split/Lip Press), a collection on short stories set in Nebraska. His fiction has been anthologized by Best Small Fictions and Best Microfiction.

John Bradley is the editor of *Atomic Ghost: Poets Respond to the Nuclear Age.* His most recent book is *Hotel Montparnasse: Letters to César Vallejo* (Dos Madres Press), a verse novel. He is the recipient of two National Endowment for the Arts Fellowships and a Pushcart Prize. A frequent book reviewer for *Rain Taxi,* he is currently a poetry editor for *Cider Press Review.*

Irish poet **Oisín Breen** is published in 95 journals in 20 countries, including *North Dakota Quarterly, The Tahoma Literary Review,* and *New Critique.* Breen's second collection, *Lilies on the Deathbed of Étaín* will be published January 2023 (Beir Bua). His debut, *'Flowers, all sorts ... '* (Dreich) drew significant praise.

Charles Brice won the 2020 Field Guide Poetry Magazine Poetry Contest and placed third in the 2021 Allen Ginsberg Poetry Prize. His fifth full-length poetry collection is *The Ventriloquist* (WordTech Editions, 2022). His poetry has been nominated twice for the Best of Net Anthology, three times for a Pushcart Prize.

Lawrence Bridges' poetry has appeared in *The New Yorker, Poetry, and The Tampa Review.* He has published three volumes of poetry: *Horses on Drums* (Red Hen Press, 2006), *Flip Days* (Red Hen Press, 2009), and *Brownwood* (Tupelo Press, 2016). You can find him on IG: @larrybridges

Stephen Campiglio directed the Mishi-maya-gat Spoken Word & Music Series for 12 years at Manchester Community College in CT. He recently served as co-editor of *Noh Place Poetry Anthology* (Lost Valley Press). Twice-nominated for a Pushcart Prize, he has published two chapbooks, *Cross-Fluence* and *Verbal Clouds through Various Magritte Skies.*

Anna Chu is a writer currently working on her novel while experiencing life outside of academia for the first time in her 22-years-of-life.

Linda Davis' short story *"The War at Home"* won the Saturday Evening Post Great American Fiction contest. Other publications: *The Iowa Review, The Literary Review, Literal Latte, Gemini Magazine,* and *Coverstory.*

Bart Edelman's poetry collections include *Crossing the Hackensack, Under Damaris' Dress, The Alphabet of Love, The Gentle Man, The Last Mojito, The Geographer's Wife,* and *Whistling to Trick the Wind.*

T.K. Edmond is a Fort Worth, Texas writer, musician, and graduate student in English at UT Arlington. T.K. is interested in dramaturgy, beauty & cruelty colliding in Texas, and general conceptualism. Work can be found in *Strukturriss, Broad River Review, The Minison Project, Abridged, Provenance Journal,* & soon in *Pidgeonholes.*

Michael Foran lives in Ware, Massachusetts, and teaches Saturday morning Literature classes at Holyoke Community College. His most recent poems have appeared in *Proud to Be: Writing by American Warriors, volume 4, Driftwood Press, Ocotillo Review* and *Rumble Fish Quarterly.*

Alfred Fournier is a writer and community volunteer in Phoenix, Arizona. His poems have appeared in *Ocotillo Review, The American Journal of Poetry, The Indianapolis Review, Welter, The Main Street Rag, Hole in the Head Review*, and elsewhere. New work is forthcoming in *Blue Unicorn* and *The Sunlight Press.*

Lynn Gilbert has had poems in *Blue Unicorn, Concho River Review, Exquisite Corpse, Gnu, The Huron River Review, Kansas Quarterly, Light, Mezzo Cammin, Mortar, Peninsula Poets,* and *Southwestern American Literature,* among others. She was a finalist in the 2021 Gerald Cable book contest.

Rosalind Goldsmith lives in Toronto and began writing short fiction seven years ago. Her stories have appeared in journals in the US, the UK and Canada, including *Litro, Filling Station, Orca, Fairlight Books, the Chiron Review* and *Fiction International.*

Benjamin Green is the author of eleven books including *The Sound of Fish Dreaming.* At the age of sixty-six he hopes his new work articulates a mature vision of the world and does so with some integrity. He resides in New Mexico.

Christine E. Hamm (she/her), queer & disabled English Professor, social worker and student of Ecopoetics, has a PhD in English. She won the Word Works Tenth Gate prize for her manuscript, Gorilla, has work featured in *NAR, Nat Brut, Painted Bride Quarterly,* and has published five books -- hybrid and poetry.

Originally from Los Angeles, **Michael Hardin** lives in rural Pennsylvania. He is the author of a chapbook from Moonstone Press (2019), has had poems published in *Seneca Review, Connecticut Review, North American Review, Quarterly West*, among others, and has been nominated for a Pushcart.

C. L. Hoang came from Vietnam in the 1970's at the end of the war. He earned his living as an engineer, until bitten by the writing bug a few years back. His writing has appeared in *The Louisville Review, Tipton Poetry Journal, Mount Hope Magazine,* and *Consequence Forum.*

Ann Howells edited *Illya's Honey* for eighteen years. Recent books: *So Long As We Speak Their Names* (Kelsay Books, 2019) and *Painting the Pinwheel Sky* (Assure Press, 2020). Chapbooks *Black Crow in Flight* and *Softly Beating Wings* were published through contests. She has windchimes in her car.

Amanda Huffman is 35 years old and lives in South Texas with her husband and two dogs. She started writing poetry as a way to process traumatic events in her life. She enjoys being in nature as much as possible, and finds adventure where she can.

Matt Ingoldby traded a Welsh sea breeze for city smog apparently by choice. His stories have been printed in the UK, USA, Canada and Australia (NZ watch this space). He works as a website manager for a UK charity.

Charles Jacobson is an army veteran with an abiding interest in philosophy and the arts and a cat who doesn't like him. He is a published author.

Karan Kapoor is in between multiple cities. Recent winner of the Red Wheelbarrow Prize & finalist for the Bellevue Literary Review Poetry Contest, his poems have appeared or are forthcoming in *Plume, Rattle, Humber Literary Review, Frontier, New Welsh Review*, & elsewhere.

Kashmiri writer **Ash Kaul** contributed a political satire column in *LITRO* and his stories were published in *Consequence, Another Chicago Magazine, The Satirist, Bella Caledonia,* and *Terrain.org.* In competitions he won: a favorite' in a Reflex Fiction Flash Fiction Competition, Montana Fiction Prize finalist, and longlisted in a Retreat West competition.

Katie King saunters past the breakfast table, allergic to the banana, avocado and egg.

Merie Kirby earned her M.F.A. from the University of Minnesota, Minneapolis. She teaches at the University of North Dakota. She is the author of two chapbooks, *The Dog Runs On* and *The Thumbelina Poems.* Her poems are featured in *Quartet Journal, Sheila-na-gig Online, West Trade Review, FERAL, Mom Egg Review, Midwest Poetry Review,* and *Avocet,* among others.

Elizabeth Kirschner is a writer and Master Gardener, living on the water in Maine. "The Story Itself," is from a novel-in-stories titled, *Learning to Hit My Mother.* She has published a collection of stories, a memoir and six volumes of poetry. She teaches at Boston College.

Paul Koniecki lives in Dallas, Texas. He was once chosen for the John Ashbery Home School Residency. His poems feature in Richard Bailey's movie "One of the Rough" distributed by AVIFF Cannes. Paul proudly sits on the editorial board of *Thimble Literary Magazine.* His poems have appeared in many journals.

Shih-Li Kow is the author of a novel and a short story collection. Her work has appeared in *Quarterly West, Mud Season Review,* and elsewhere. She lives in Kuala Lumpur and dreams of road trips.

Scott Lowery is a poet, musician, retired educator, and recent transplant from rural Minnesota to the Milwaukee area. His new chapbook, *Mutual Life* (Finishing Line, summer 2023), bears witness to turbulent times. Recent work appears in current issues of *Pinyon, River Styx, Nimrod, Bramble,* and *RockPa-*

perPoem.

Rowan MacDonald lives in Tasmania with his dog, Rosie. His writing has appeared in *Black Fork Review, White Wall Review, Miracle Monocle, Sheepshead Review, Defunkt Magazine, FLARE: The Flagler Review* and *Stereo Stories*. His work has also been adapted into short film by New Form Digital.

Shannan Mann is an Indian-Canadian poet. Recent winner of the Peatsmoke Summer Contest & finalist for the 2022 Rattle Poetry Prize & 2021 Frontier Award for New Poets, she has poems in *Rattle, Birdcoat Quarterly, Frontier, Humber Literary Review, Oh Reader* & elsewhere.

Jennifer MacKenzie's first book of poems, *My Not-My Soldier,* was published as part of Fence Books' Modern Poets Series. Her poems have appeared in numerous journals, most recently *Jubilat, Image, Prelude,* and *Conduit.* She lives in the Bronx and teaches at Lehman College, CUNY.

James Mathis has been published by *Flash Fiction Magazine, WMG Publishing, the Dribble Drabble Review* and others. He lives in Dallas area with his wife and their superhero rescue dog Saber-Girl. James earned his MFA from Lindenwood University in Spring, 2022, serving as editorial assistant for the *Lindenwood Review.*

Richard L. Matta grew up in New York's Hudson Valley, practiced forensic science, and now lives in San Diego with his golden-doodle dog. Some of his work is found in *Ancient Paths, Dewdrop, San Pedro River Review, New Verse News*, and many haiku journals.

Jen McClanaghan's work has appeared in numerous journals including *The New Yorker, The Iowa Review, The Southern Review, New England Review,* and in *Best American Poetry.*

Robert McGuill's work has appeared in *Narrative, the Southwest Review, Louisiana Literature, American Fiction* and other publications. His stories have been nominated for the Pushcart Prize on five occasions, and short-listed for awards by, among others, *Glimmer Train, the New Guard, Sequestrum Art & Literature.*

Bruce McRae, a Canadian musician, is a multiple Pushcart nominee with poems published in hundreds of magazines such as *Poetry, Rattle* and the *North American Review.*

In November of 2022 **R.w. Meeks** won the Palm Beach Book Festival contest for 'Best Writer in Palm Beach" and in January 2023 his manuscript "The Dream Collector" was chosen as Runner-Up in the contest sponsored by the Historical Fiction Company for "Best Historical Fiction Novel of 2022"

Over 150 of **Tom Misuraca**'s short stories and two novels have been published. This year, his work has appeared in *SIAMB! (Something Involving A MailBox), Literature Today* and *Roi Fainéant.* Last year, his story, "Giving Up The Ghosts", was published in *Constellations Journal,* and nominated for a Pushcart Prize.

Eva Nemirovsky is a young writer, recently graduated from UC Davis, who lives with her cat and her partner in Davis. She enjoys playing Dungeons and Dragons, rock climbing, and drawing in her free time.

Donna Obeid's work has appeared in *Carve Magazine, Detroit Metropolitan Woman, Flash Fiction Magazine, Hawai'i Pacific Review, The Malibu Times,* and is forthcoming in *South 85 Journal.* She lives in Palo Alto, California.

Cassady O'Reilly-Hahn is a poet with an MA from Claremont Graduate University. He is an editor for *Foothill: A Poetry Journal* and he works for Deluxe, a company that localizes TV and Film. Cassady writes Haiku for his Instagram @cassady_orha. He currently resides in Redlands, California.

Christian Paulisich is an undergraduate poet at Johns Hopkins University. He lives in Baltimore, Maryland, but is originally from the Bay Area, California. His poems have appeared in *Neologism Poetry Journal, Orchards Poetry Journal, Beltway Poetry Quarterly,* and *Monterey Poetry Review.*

Karlie Powers has a bachelor's degree in English Literature and Composition. She's a public school teacher by day; and a student of The Writers Studio by night. She currently lives in Tucson with her partner and dog.

Daniel A. Rabuzzi has had two novels, five short stories, twenty poems, and nearly 50 essays / articles published. He lives in New York City with his artistic partner & spouse, the woodcarver Deborah A. Mills.

Greta Rasmus is a poet based in Texas, where she spends her time tending to her craft and her community. Her work has been featured in the *Winter Storm Project,* in group texts to girlfriends, in zoom rooms with giving writers and readers and on porches with people she loves.

M. Ann Reed offers the Bio-Poetic Study of Literature supporting the Deep

Ecology Movement for global and local students, some of whom publish. *Antithesis, Azure, Burningword, EI Review, Kallisto Gaia, Parabola, Poeming Pigeon, Proverse Hong Kong,* and *Psychological Perspectives* are home to her poems. FLP published her chapbook, *making oxygen.*

Pete Riebling lives in Metuchen, New Jersey with his wife, daughter and son and their cat, Mrs. Kisses, and their dog, Opal.

Janice Rodriguez is published in *Please See Me, Evening Street Review, The Ocotillo Review, The Writing Disorder, The Copperfield Review, JONAH magazine,* and *The Indiana Voice Journal.* When not writing, she's in the garden, moving her perennials around as if they were furniture, or in the kitchen, working her way through a stack of cookbooks.

Jim Ross jumped into creative pursuits in 2015 after a rewarding research career. He's since published nonfiction, fiction, poetry, photography, plays, and hybrid in 175 journals on five continents. Publications include *Burningword, Columbia Journal, Hippocampus, Kestrel, Newfound, Stonecoast, The Atlantic,* and *Typehouse.* Jim and family split time between city and mountains.

Claire Rubin is an award-winning poet who has received multiple Pushcart Prize nominations. Her work has appeared in the *Atlanta Review, Bellevue Literary Review, New Ohio Review, Enizagam* and *Healing Muse* among others. Claire is the author of *Waiting to be Called* and *Until I Couldn't.*

Ashley Robles (Schmidt) is an artist currently residing in San Antonio, TX, a UT Austin alum, and is working to normalize chronic illness in her corporate & creative life.

Hilary Sideris's most recent book *Liberty Laundry* (Dos Madres Press 2022) was recommended by Small Press Distribution. She lives in Brooklyn, NY.

Leah Skay is a twenty-three-year-old writer and aspiring graduate student from rural Delaware, currently living in rural Japan as a middle-school English teacher. She is an avid true crime consumer, bee enthusiast, and Sendai City sweets endorser.

Jane Snyder's stories have appeared in *Red Rock, Two Hawks* and *Frigg.* She lives in Spokane.

Anthony St. George lives in San Francisco with his husband. His flash, speculative, and experimental fiction appears in such publications as *New Maps,*

Ligeia Magazine, and *streetcake magazine.*

Peter J. Stavros is a writer in Louisville, Kentucky, and the author of the short story collection, Three in the Morning and You Don't Smoke Anymore (Etchings Press).

Jacob R. Weber is a translator living in Maryland. He has published fiction in *The Bellevue Literary Review, New Letters, The Baltimore Review, The Chattahoochee Review,* and other journals. His book of short stories, *"Don't Wait to Be Called,"* won the 2017 Washington Writers' Publishing House Award for Fiction.

JULIA DARLING MEMORIAL
POETRY PRIZE
WINNER RECEIVES $1200. 2ND PLACE $100
SUBMISSIONS OPEN: May 1
SUBMISSIONS CLOSE: Midnight August 20

The Julia Darling Memorial Poetry Prize winner will be published in The Ocotillo Review Volume 8.1

>All entrants will receive a copy of the journal and be considered for publication.

>Submit 1-3 poems in a single document per entry. Begin each poem on a separate page. Limit poems to 65 lines including title and spaces. Entries should not exceed 10 pages.

>There is a $20.00 fee per entry. Poets may submit multiple entries by paying additional entry fees.

>Do not put your name or other identifying info on the document or in the submission title.

>We welcome the expression of diverse voices, diverse cultures, including poems partly or entirely in languages other than English. Please include an English translation.

>No previously published poems - print or online - will be accepted. This includes poems posted on personal websites or social network pages or groups.

>We will accept simultaneous submissions for the Julia Darling Memorial Poetry Prize with the understanding that any poem published elsewhere will be withdrawn immediately.

More info available at:
www.kallistogaiapress.org

SUBMISSIONS FOR THE ANNUAL

ACACIA FICTION PRIZE

WINNER RECEIVES $1500 AND PUBLICATION
Plus - 20 copies & 20 press packs to reviewers

SUBMISSIONS OPEN: September 15
SUBMISSIONS CLOSE: December 31

Guidelines:

> The entry fee is $25.
> All entrants will receive a copy of the winning collection.
> Submit any combination of short stories, flash fiction, and/ or novellas totalling 30K to 60K words. Longer works may be considered but limit your submission to 60K words. Novels will not be accepted for this contest.
> Do not put your name or any identifying markings, including an acknowledgements page, in the body or title of the submission.
> All submissions received through Submittable.
> We adhere to the ethical standards suggested by the Community of Literary Magazines and Publishers (CLMP).

More info available at:
www.kallistogaiapress.org

SAGUARO POETRY PRIZE

WINNER RECEIVES $1500 AND PUBLICATION
Plus - 20 copies & 20 press packs to reviewers

SUBMISSIONS OPEN: SEPTEMBER 15
SUBMISSIONS CLOSE: DECEMBER 31

Guidelines:

> The entry fee is $25.
> All entrants will receive a copy of the winning chapbook.
> Submit 28 to 48 pages of contemporary poetry.
> Do not put your name or any identifying markings, including an acknowledgements page, in the body or title of the submission.
> All submissions received through Submittable.
> We adhere to the ethical standards suggested by the Community of Literary Magazines and Publishers (CLMP).

More info available at:

www.kallistogaiapress.org

Joshua Tree Novel Prize

Submissions open: January 1
Submissions close: May 31
Winner Receives $2000 and publication
Plus - 20 copies & 20 press packs to reviewers

Guidelines:

> The entry fee is $70.
> All entrants will receive a +/- 800 word critique / analysis of their entry from our editorial staff
> All entrants will receive a copy of the winning novel.
> All finalists will be considered for publication.
> Submit the first 10,000 words of your completed manuscript plus a synopsis of no more than 2500 words
> Do not put your name or any identifying markings, in the body or title of the submission.
> All submissions received through Submittable.
> We adhere to the ethical standards suggested by the Community of Literary Magazines and Publishers (CLMP). Finalists will be selected using a double-concealed reading.
> The editorial staff of Kallisto Gaia Press will select five finalists to forward to the guest judge.

More info available at:
www.kallistogaiapress.org